ASSET & LIABILITY
MANAGEMENT

Prentice Hall
FINANCIAL TIMES

In an increasingly competitive world, we believe it's quality of thinking that will give you the edge – an idea that opens new doors, a technique that solves a problem, or an insight that simply makes sense of it all. The more you know, the smarter and faster you can go.

That's why we work with the best minds in business and finance to bring cutting-edge thinking and best learning practice to a global market.

Under a range of leading imprints, including Financial Times Prentice Hall, we create world-class print publications and electronic products bringing our readers knowledge, skills and understanding which can be applied whether studying or at work.

To find out more about our business publications, or tell us about the books you'd like to find, you can visit us at www.business-minds.com

For other Pearson Education publications, visit www.pearsoned-ema.com

ASSET & LIABILITY MANAGEMENT

A GUIDE TO
VALUE CREATION AND RISK CONTROL

JEAN DERMINE AND YOUSSEF F. BISSADA

With the collaboration of
E. MERCIER AND N. GUEGAN

What every banker, central banker, banks' auditors,
consultants and lawyers
need to know

FINANCIAL TIMES

An imprint of Pearson Education

London • New York • Toronto • Sydney • Tokyo • Singapore • Hong Kong
Cape Town • New Delhi • Madrid • Paris • Amsterdam • Munich • Milan • Stockholm

PEARSON EDUCATION LIMITED

Head Office:
Edinburgh Gate
Harlow CM20 2JE
Tel: +44 (0)1279 623623
Fax: +44 (0)1279 431059

London Office:
128 Long Acre
London WC2E 9AN
Tel: +44 (0)20 7447 2000
Fax: +44 (0)20 4472170
Website: www.financialminds.com

First published in Great Britain in 2002

ISBN 0 273 65656 2

British Library Cataloguing in Publication Data
A CIP catalogue record for this book can be obtained from the British Library

10   9   8   7   6   5   4

Designed by Claire Brodmann Book Designs, Lichfield, Staffs
Typeset by Pantek Arts Ltd, Maidstone, Kent
Printed and bound in Great Britain by Biddles Ltd., Guildford and Kings Lynn

The Publishers' policy is to use paper manufactured from sustainable forests.

To Isabelle, Nicolas, Martin, Suzanne, Alexandre,
Augustin and Juliette

To Hoda and Joanna

ABOUT THE AUTHORS

Jean Dermine is Professor of Banking and Finance at INSEAD, Fontainebleau. With more than 20 years of research and consulting in the field of asset and liability management, he has directed programmes for bankers in Europe, the Americas, Africa, Japan, South-East Asia and the Middle East. Jean Dermine has been Visiting Professor at the Wharton School of the University of Pennsylvania, at the Universities of Lausanne and Louvain, at the Stockholm School of Economics, and a Visiting Fellow at New York University Salomon Center. He is Director of the INSEAD Center in International Financial Services (CIFS) and the co-author of the banking simulation ALCO Challenge.

Youssef F. Bissada is owner and chairman of Bissada Management Simulations, a company specializing in the development of computer-aided educational packages and strategic planning softwares. He started his career at INSEAD in 1969 where he teaches in both the MBA and executive development programmes. He works as a consultant for numerous international organizations and corporations in Europe, Asia, Africa and the USA. Apart from his research in the fields of international operations, project management and transfer of technology, Professor Bissada is the author of the business simulation SIGMA Challenge.

CONTENTS

Acknowledgments   viii

Introduction   ix

Stage 1   Banking services and balance sheet   1

Stage 2   Value creation for shareholders   5

Stage 3   ROE breakdown   11

Stage 4   Profit centre management   19

Stage 5   Profit allocation and transfer pricing for deposits and loans   25

Stage 6   The capital adequacy regulation   35

Stage 7   Loan pricing (1): the 'equity' spread   43

Stage 8   Loan pricing (2): credit risk and credit provisions   51

Stage 9   Securitization   59

Stage 10   Value creation: a summary   65

Stage 11   The control of interest rate risk (1): the repricing gaps   69

Stage 12   The control of interest rate risk (2): the simulation model   77

Stage 13   Forwards and financial futures   83

Stage 14   The control of interest rate risk (3): the value of equity at risk   91

Stage 15   The control of liquidity risk   97

Stage 16   Options   101

Stage 17   Asset and liability management: an art, not a science   107

Appendix A: Software   113

Appendix B: Answers to exercises   117

Appendix C: Glossary   135

Appendix D: References   147

Index   151

ACKNOWLEDGMENTS

This book grows out of 20 years' banking research and training of bankers in Europe, the Americas, Africa and Asia. As deregulation and competition are reducing margins around the world, the need for knowledge on Asset and Liability Management, the control of bank's profit and risks, becomes an absolute necessity for any banker in charge of a profit centre, central bankers in charge of bank supervision, and banks' auditors, consultants or lawyers.

Being often very specialized, bankers rarely have an opportunity to master the control of profit and risk of an entire bank. This is the purpose of this book, written for bankers working in retail banking, corporate and institutional banking or treasury, as well as for central bankers and banks' auditors or lawyers. The pedagogy is unique for three major reasons:

- First, it provides two self-contained vehicles with exercises: a book and a software. The paper-based version offers a more in-depth explanation of the concepts, while the computer version relies more on visual intuition.

- Second, it not only covers the control of interest rate and liquidity risks but also provides a complete coverage of shareholder value creation, loan pricing, loan provisioning and securitization.

- Third, building on a very large executive education experience, it emphasizes the intuition, relying on mathematics only where necessary.

The authors acknowledge the patience and comments of the many bankers and MBA students in Europe, North America, Latin America, Africa and Asia who have tested the ALM concepts and exercises. They acknowledge the interpersonal skills of Nathalie Guegan, manager of the project at Bissada Management Simulations, the creativity of Eric Escoffier in designing the computer animations, and the outstanding software expertise of Etienne Mercier. Developed over 20 years, Etienne's expertise has helped to translate a professor's message and dream into a computerized reality. Finally, the authors acknowledge the creative environment at INSEAD, a global business school where the rigour of academic research meets effort for relevant classroom delivery.

July 2001 Fontainebleau

INTRODUCTION

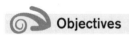

Objectives

The purpose of this book is to study asset and liability management (ALM) of a commercial bank. ALM includes a set of tools that ensure that value is created for shareholders and that risks are being put under control.

The pedagogy is unique, with two self-contained vehicles: a book and a software.

As the banking world is shifting from an overriding concern for balance sheet expansion to a preoccupation with rates of return on capital and risk control, knowledge of ALM is becoming a necessity for all bankers accountable for the results of a profit centre. *Asset & Liability Management* is designed for corporate bankers, treasurers, heads of retail branches, ALM specialist, and bank strategic planners. Central bankers, auditors, consultants or lawyers will also appreciate the relevance of the book.

Starting from the basics and going into more advanced issues, this book provides complete coverage of asset and liability management. As the course moves along step by step, no previous knowledge of ALM is needed.

Although tools could be introduced in a complex mathematical manner, the presentation in the book is kept intuitive and simple by using modern visual educational techniques.

 Contents

Asset & Liability Management incorporates the modern techniques used in profitability and risk management of a commercial bank. Five interrelated topics will be discussed:

- shareholder value creation;
- profit centre management;
- risk-adjusted performance management;
- pricing credit risk and loan provisioning;
- the management of interest rate and liquidity risks.

 The learning methods

Very much as the *Tour de France* takes cyclists stage by stage to the Champs Elysées in Paris, *Asset & Liability Management* is divided into 17 stages represented on a map. This progressive course will enable you to fully understand specific concepts and tools, and working through exercises will reinforce your knowledge acquisition.

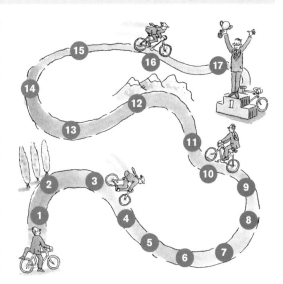

Each stage introduces new information, building on the learning from the previous one. Each stage consists of three main parts:

- An introduction of new concepts.

- A chapter summary (key points).

- Exercises.

According to your personal preference you will use:

- the paper-based modular version;
- the computer version;
- a combination of both.

Both paper and computer versions follow each other closely in content and structure. Each is self-contained. The paper-based version offers a more in-depth explanation of the concepts, while the computer version relies more on visual intuition. Experience has shown that the consecutive use of the two vehicles, paper-based or software, does help to reinforce the understanding and mastery of ALM. Information on how to install and use the software can be found in Appendix A.

Whichever version you decide to use, we recommend that you check your answers as you work through exercises. You will find the answers at the end of the book or within the computer software. When entering the answers to an exercise in the software, you can click on the magnifying-glass button to verify the answer. A green colour indicates that it is correct; a red colour indicates an error. If you click on the light bulb, the computer will show you how to calculate the correct answer.

The learning methods are based on self-study techniques and the course is designed to be completed in whichever way suits you best. Trials have suggested that it is usually more efficient to complete the materials in short 'chunks' of a few stages at a time.

You may decide to team up with a 'learning partner' a colleague who will go through the course with you and with whom you could share and comment on viewpoints. This approach works equally well in small groups.

Your organization may nominate a 'mentor' to guide you through the learning.

BANKING SERVICES
AND BALANCE SHEET

You have just been hired by e-Bank as chief financial officer (CFO). One of your main tasks is to supervise the asset and liability management system that is the control of profitability and risks at e-Bank. On your first day at work, you would like to know more about the activities of e-Bank and you ask for the latest annual report.

Flows of funds in banking

e-Bank is a regular commercial bank. Two of its main functions are to collect deposits and to lend money. Its clients can be households (the retail market), firms (the corporate market) or the public sector.

e-Bank is also dealing with other commercial banks on the interbank market, the place where banks lend or borrow from one another. The interbank lending rate is called the *ask* rate, while the interbank borrowing rate is called the *bid* rate.

Finally, in many countries, banks are required to maintain a fixed percentage of their deposits in an account with the central bank. This is called the reserve requirement (Figure 1.1).

The balance sheet of e-Bank is a picture of the company at a specific date, which shows you the sources of funds (liabilities and shareholders' equity) and the uses of funds (assets). The simplified balance sheet presented here will be the one used throughout the book.

Figure 1.1 The flow of funds in banking

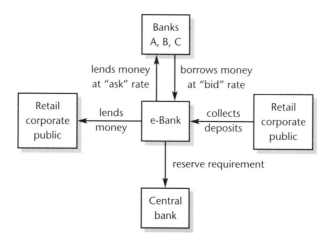

Balance sheet (31 December, 2000) $ million

Assets		Liabilities and shareholders' equity	
Reserves with central bank	40	Deposits	800
Loans	500	Interbank deposits	200
Interbank loans	300		
Government bonds	230	Equity	100
Fixed assets	30		
Total	1100	Total	1100

You will notice that the equity of a commercial bank is a small part of the sources of funds, while the fixed assets (buildings and equipment, computers) are a small part of total assets. A large part of the funds are deposits collected from customers and/or money borrowed from other banks. Three large categories of assets include loans to customers, loans to other banks or a portfolio of government bonds.

Banks also engage in off-balance sheet operations or contingent claims. These are contracts whereby two parties agree to exchange cash in the future if some event occurs. For instance, imagine that a company is borrowing from local investors. To reassure investors that they will be repaid, the company could negotiate with e-Bank a *stand by* agreement. The bank promises to *stand by* (i.e. deliver cash to investors) if the company is unable to honour its obligation, i.e. to repay investors. As at the time of origination of the *stand by* the contract does not yet have any impact on assets or liabilities (with the exception of the fee paid to the bank), it is referred to as an *off-balance sheet* transaction. Some of these contracts will be discussed in Stages 13 and 16.

 ## Asset and liability management

To control profitability and risks, banks have set up an asset liability committee (ALCO). It usually includes the very senior management of the bank: president, chief financial officer, head of treasury, head of retail banking, head of corporate banking, chief economist, and head of accounting and control. Some banks refer to this committee as GALCO (group asset liability committee) or ALMAC (asset liability management and action committee). Although the tasks involved – profit and risk control – are not new, the allocation of information, responsibility and accountability to the very senior management is a more recent phenomenon, imposed by the central bank in some countries. As deregulation and competition are reducing margins around the world, the need for more precise information and a complete asset and liability management system becomes an absolute necessity.

KEY POINTS

➡ Banks have three main sources of funds: deposits collected from clients, interbank deposits and shareholders' equity.

➡ Banks invest in five major assets: reserves with the central bank, loans, interbank loans, bonds and fixed assets.

➡ The asset liability committee (ALCO) controls profit and risks. It includes the president and the heads of business units, such as retail, corporate and treasury.

VALUE CREATION FOR
SHAREHOLDERS

Since your appointment, your sister has purchased some equity issued by the bank. As the shares of e-Bank are listed for the first time on the stock exchange, you are curious to see the share price and the market value of the equity purchased by your sister.

If the share price of a company is too high, investors will not be willing to buy the shares as their return will be too low. Conversely, if the share price is very low, it will be a bargain and all investors will hurry to buy these shares.

As a consequence, a fair price should offer investors a decent return. What is it?

To answer this very important question, we need to consider the investment opportunities available to investors.

The two types of investment opportunities available to your sister and other shareholders include the following:

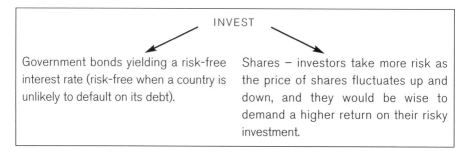

INVEST	
Government bonds yielding a risk-free interest rate (risk-free when a country is unlikely to default on its debt).	Shares – investors take more risk as the price of shares fluctuates up and down, and they would be wise to demand a higher return on their risky investment.

The difference between the expected return on a risky share and the risk-free rate on government bonds is called the *risk premium*.

In other words, the expected return on a bank share will be equal to the current interest rate on bonds plus a risk premium.

Expected return on a bank share = Risk-free rate on bonds + risk premium

The expected return on a share is sometimes referred to as the *average* return. As the share price goes up and down, the return on your investment can be high or low. The expected return is the *average* of these high and low returns.

In the OECD (Organization for Economic Co-operation and Development) countries, the estimates of the risk premium for commercial banks' shares range between 4% and 6%. For instance, if the interest rate on government bonds is 10% and the risk premium on bank shares is 5%, then

Expected return on a bank share = 10% + 5% = 15%

The expected return on a bank share is sometimes called the cost of equity (COE). It represents an *opportunity* cost for the shareholders of e-Bank as they could take the money and invest in other shares traded on the stock market. The cost of equity is the rate used by the stock market to compute the value of bank shares.

Valuation of bank shares

Let us take the example of e-Bank.

We know that the equity invested by shareholders in e-Bank is equal to $100 million (see balance sheet in Stage 1). Imagine that the stock market expects e-Bank to generate a steady annual profit after tax of $10.8 million, paid every year as a dividend.

The return on equity (ROE = profit/equity = 10.8/100) of e-Bank is 10.8%.

To simplify the example and avoid unnecessary mathematics, imagine that the bank is closed after three years, and that investors, your sister included, recover their initial equity investment of $100 million. The timing of the dividends accruing to investors is as follows:

	Year 1	Year 2	Year 3
Cash flow (dividends) to investors	+10.8	+10.8	+10.8 + 100

Two cases will be considered:

1. In the first case, the stock market demands a 5% return on its investment.
2. In the second case, the market demands a 15% return.

CASE 1 5% DISCOUNT RATE

As is the case for any financial instrument traded on mature financial markets, the value of the bank shares is the discounted value of the future cash flows paid to the investors. The discount rate is the return demanded by the market, that is the cost of equity:

$$\text{Market value of shares (@ 5\%)} = \frac{10.8}{(1.05)^1} + \frac{10.8}{(1.05)^2} + \frac{110.8}{(1.05)^3} = 115.8$$

☺ In this example, the market value of shares (115.8) exceeds the equity (100) invested by shareholders. GOOD NEWS for your sister and the shareholders: value has been created!

The difference between the market value of the shares and the equity investment is called the value creation.

Value creation = market value of shares – equity investment
$$= 115.8 - 100 = 15.8$$

CASE 2 15% DISCOUNT RATE

We are still considering e-Bank with a return on equity of 10.8%. But now imagine that the stock market demands a return of 15%.

Again, the market value of shares is the discounted value of future dividends:

$$\text{Market value of shares (@ 15\%)} = \frac{10.8}{(1.15)^1} + \frac{10.8}{(1.15)^2} + \frac{110.8}{(1.15)^3} = 90.4$$

☹ The shareholders' initial equity investment of 100 is valued at only 90.4 by the stock market. BAD NEWS for your sister and the shareholders: value has been destroyed!

Value destruction = market value – equity investment = 90.4 – 100 = – 9.6

Your sister would have been better off avoiding this equity investment.

The two cases can be summarized in Table 2.1.

Table 2.1 The outcome of different discount rates

Equity invested = 100	Year 1	Year 2	Year 3	Market Value	Value creation (destruction)	Shareholder satisfaction
Cash flows	10.8	10.8	110.8			
Case I: market value at 5%	$10.8/1.05$	$10.8/(1.05)^2$	$110.8/(1.05)^3$	115.8	15.8	☺
Case 2: market value at 15%	$10.8/1.15$	$10.8/(1.15)^2$	$110.8/(1.15)^3$	90.4	–9.6	☹

Managerial rules

Two managerial rules can be deduced from this simple example.

1. Value is created for shareholders as long as the market value (MV) of shares exceeds the value of equity invested:

Value creation if market value (MV) > equity invested

The ALM process of a bank will have to ensure that managerial decisions lead to value creation, a management style referred to as *value-based management*.

2. You can easily check that the market value of shares will exceed the equity investment of 100 when the ROE of e-Bank exceeds the discount rate used by the stock market. In case 1, the ROE of 10.8% exceeds the discount rate of 5% and there is a value creation of 15.8. In case 2, the ROE of 10.8% is below the discount rate of 15% and there is a value destruction of –9.6.

Thus a golden rule for value creation is that the ROE of e-Bank must be larger than the discount rate (the cost of equity) to ensure value creation.

ROE > cost of equity = risk-free rate + risk premium

9

> **KEY POINTS**
>
> ➡ Shareholder value is created when the market value of shares exceeds the equity invested.
>
> ➡ The cost of equity is the minimum return demanded by shareholders.
>
> ➡ Cost of equity = risk-free rate on bonds + risk premium.
>
> ➡ Value is created when ROE > cost of equity.

EXERCISE STAGE TWO

Consider a bank with an initial equity of 100, an ROE of 10%, and a life of three years. The profit is paid every year as a dividend plus a closing dividend of 110 at the end of three years. Compute the market value and value creation for the cases when the market discounts at 12%, 10% and 8%.

	Year 1	Year 2	Year 3
Cash flow accruing to investors	10	10	110

Please fill in the blanks:

a) Market value at 12% $= \dfrac{\dots}{(1+\dots)} + \dfrac{\dots}{(1+\dots)^2} + \dfrac{\dots}{(1+\dots)^3} = \dots$

    Value creation $= \dots - 100 = \dots$

b) Market value at 10% $= \dfrac{\dots}{(1+\dots)} + \dfrac{\dots}{(1+\dots)^2} + \dfrac{\dots}{(1+\dots)^3} = \dots$

    Value creation $= \dots - 100 = \dots$

c) Market value at 8% $= \dfrac{\dots}{(1+\dots)} + \dfrac{\dots}{(1+\dots)^2} + \dfrac{\dots}{(1+\dots)^3} = \dots$

    Value creation $= \dots - 100 = \dots$

Managerial lesson: to create value, the ROE must exceed the market discount rate, the cost of equity.

ROE BREAKDOWN

As we noticed in Stage 2, the value of shares will be affected by the future profitability and return on equity of e-Bank. A large ROE is likely to lead to a higher valuation.

As the chief financial officer of e-Bank, you want to understand what are the major economic drivers of the return on equity.

To analyze the ROE, you will need both the bank's income statement and the balance sheet.

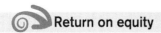
Return on equity

Let us first introduce e-Bank's income statement. The income statement of a company shows the change in the wealth of shareholders (the equity) over a specific period of time.

Income statement ($ million), 2000

	Interest income	90	Interest earned on loans and bonds
+	Fees from services	30	Commissions from services (ex: credit card fees...)
−	Interest expenses	−70	Interest paid on deposits
−	Provisions for bad debt	−10	Provisions for losses on loans
−	Operating expenses	−22	Non-interest expenses such as wages, computers
	Profit before tax	18	
−	Corporate tax (40%)	− 7.2	
	Profit after tax	10.8	

e-Bank's balance sheet is similar to the one presented in Stage One.

Balance sheet ($ million), 31 December 2000

Assets	Liabilities
1100	Debt: 1000 (including deposits)
	Equity: 100

The return on equity is the ratio of the profit after tax divided by the equity:

ROE = profit after tax/equity = 10.8 / 100 = 10.8%

A reading of the income statement shows that the profit after tax is a result of the revenue from assets, the cost of funds, the level of operating expenses and corporate taxes. As we show below, these variables lead to financial ratios which are the major economic drivers of e-Bank's return on equity.

a) The average earnings-on-assets (EOA) calculated as:

EOA = (interest income + fees − provisions)/total assets

EOA = (90 + 30 − 10) / 1100 = 10%

As the term indicates, the earnings-on-assets ratio measures the average revenue per dollar of asset.[1]

b) The average cost of debt (COD) calculated as:

COD = interest expenses/total debt

COD = 70 / 1000 = 7%

The cost of debt measures the average cost of funds, that is the interest expense per dollar of debt.

c) The average operating expenses (OE) ratio calculated as:

OE ratio = operating expenses/total assets

OE = 22 /1100 = 2%

This ratio indicates the level of non-interest expense per dollar of assets. As banking is a service industry, a large part of these expenses includes wages.[2]

d) The average corporate tax rate (t) calculated as:

Average tax rate (t) = taxes/profit before tax

t = 7.2 / 18 = 40%

---

[1] When the volume of assets changes substantially over the year, it is recommended that revenues are divided by the average assets of the year.

[2] Bank analysts often refer to another expense ratio, the cost-income ratio (also called the efficiency ratio). It is defined as the ratio of operating expenses divided by gross revenue (interest income plus fees minus interest expenses). This ratio indicates the part of revenue that is absorbed by operating expenses. One major drawback of this ratio to serve as a measure of cost control is that it is affected not only by costs but also by revenue.

c) The leverage or gearing of e-Bank defined as:

Leverage = debt/equity

Leverage =1000/ 100 = 10

These five financial variables drive the ROE through the following relationship (a proof is included in the Note). The ROE is the sum of two parts:

ROE = (EOA – OE) x (1 – t) + (EOA – COD – OE) x (debt/equity) × (1 – t)

| In the first part, you find the EOA net of operating expenses (OE) × the tax factor (1– t) | The second part is made of the product of three terms: The margin (EOA – COD) net of operating expenses × leverage (debt/equity) × tax factor (1 – t) |

If we apply the above formula to e-Bank, the ROE can be broken down as follows:

ROE =   (10% – 2%) × (1 – 40%)
+ (10% – 7% – 2%) × (100/10) × (1 – 40%)
= 4. 8% + 6% = 10.8%

This leads to the conclusion that five key variables drive the return on equity of e-Bank (Figure 3.1).

Figure 3.1 **The five key variables driving e-Bank's ROE**

ROE
- Earnings on assets (EOA)
- Margin (EOA – COD)
- Operating expense (OE)
- Leverage (debt/equity)
- Tax (t)

Since leverage (debt/equity) can have a major impact on the ROE of a bank, there is a temptation to reduce equity and increase debt. In order to put a limit to leverage, central banks have devised regulations on capital adequacy (see Stage 6).

➡ **The ROE can be broken down into a set of five economic drivers:**

ROE $= (EOA - OE) \times (1 - t)$

      $+ (EOA - COD - OE) \times (debt/equity) \times (1 - t)$

EOA   = (interest income + fees − provisions)/total assets

OE ratio = Operating expenses/total assets

Margin   = EOA − COD

Leverage = debt/equity

Tax   = t

 Note: ROE breakdown

Let us assume that:

A = Total assets

D = Total debt

E = equity

EOA = Earnings on assets

COD = Cost of debt

OE = Operating expenses

t = Corporate tax rate

$$ROE = \text{Profit after tax/equity} = ((EOA \times A - OE \times A - COD \times D) \times (1-t))/E$$
$$= ((EOA - OE) \times A - COD \times D) \times (1-t))/E$$
$$= ((EOA - OE) \times (E + D) - COD \times D) \times (1-t)/E$$
$$= (EOA - OE) \times (1-t)$$
$$+ (EOA - COD - OE) \times D/E \times (1-t)$$

EXERCISE STAGE THREE

The balance sheet and income statement of your bank are as follows:

Balance sheet (end of the year, $ million)

Assets	110	Debt (including deposits)	105
		Equity	5
Total	110	Total	110

Income statement ($ million)

Interest income	8.2
Fees	0.8
− Interest expenses	− 5.25
− Provisions for bad debts	− 1.3
− Operating expenses	− 1.1
Profit before tax	1.35
− Taxes	− 0.54
Profit after tax	0.81

Please compute the following ratios:

Return on equity $= \dfrac{\ldots\ldots}{\ldots\ldots} = \ldots\ldots$

Earnings on assets $= \dfrac{(\ldots\ldots + \ldots\ldots - \ldots\ldots)}{\ldots\ldots} = \ldots\ldots$

Cost of debt $= \dfrac{\ldots\ldots}{\ldots\ldots} = \ldots\ldots$

Operating expenses ratio $= \dfrac{\ldots\ldots}{\ldots\ldots} = \ldots\ldots$

Leverage (D/E) $= \dfrac{\ldots\ldots}{\ldots\ldots} = \ldots\ldots$

Tax rate $= \dfrac{\ldots\ldots}{\ldots\ldots} = \ldots\ldots$

Verify that:

ROE = (profit after tax)/(equity) = ... / ...... = ...

ROE = (EOA − OE) × (1−t)   + (EOA − COD − OE) × (D/E) × (1−t)

    = ((..... − .....) × (1 − .....)) + ((..... − ...... − .....) × (.....) × (1 − ......))

    = ... + ... = ...

PROFIT CENTRE MANAGEMENT

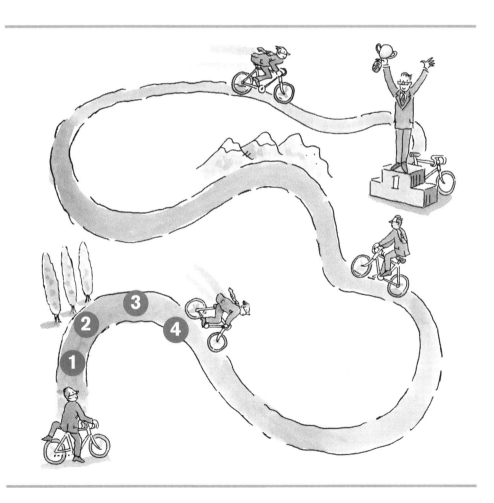

We have discussed the concept of value creation and the need for e-Bank to achieve a satisfactory return on equity.

Value creation and ROE are useful tools to evaluate the overall performance of e-Bank. However, as the newly appointed CFO, you need to know which business units of e-Bank create value and which ones require intensive care.

e-Bank is a complex organization that can be visualized as the sum of several business units. We are going to assess separately the profitability of each of these profit centres.

A profit centre could be a specific branch in London, it could be the business unit servicing retail customers, the corporate bank, the treasury department ...

RAROC, EVA, economic profit

In Stage 3, we calculated the return on equity of e-Bank:

ROE = profit after tax/equity.

For simplicity, we can visualize profit after tax and equity as two pies (Figure 4.1).

The pies are divided into pieces which represent the allocated amount of profit or equity to a particular business unit. For instance, the profit after tax allocated to business A is 2, while the amount of equity allocated to business A is 10.

With these profit and equity allocations, we can compute the return on equity of a specific profit centre. Many banks call this return RAROC, the risk-adjusted return on capital:

RAROC = allocated profit/allocated equity

For instance, the RAROC of profit centre A is: 2/10 = 20%.

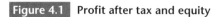

Figure 4.1 Profit after tax and equity

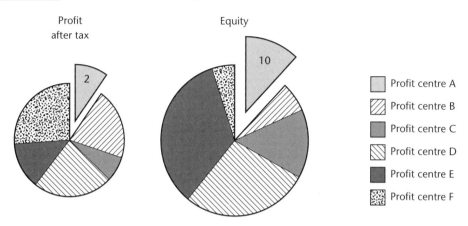

With reference to Stage two, the golden rule of value creation requires that the RAROC of a profit centre be larger than the cost of equity of e-Bank, the opportunity return available to investors on financial markets.

RAROC > cost of equity

For instance, if the cost of equity of e-Bank is 15%, then profit centre A meets the golden rule: RAROC = 20% > cost of equity = 15%

Since RAROC is expressed in a percentage format that ignores the size of the business unit and the actual amount of value created, there is another useful management concept tool called the economic profit or economic value added (EVA™). This is the difference between the allocated profit of a business unit and its cost of equity:

EVA   **= allocated profit after tax – cost of allocated equity**

   = allocated profit after tax – (allocated equity × cost of equity).

For instance, the EVA of profit centre A is: EVA = 2 – (15% × 10) = 0.5

Economic profit or EVA simply reminds managers that the creation of value does not only require a positive profit. It also demands a profit exceeding the cost of allocated equity, that is the expected revenue that shareholders could obtain themselves in simply buying other bank shares traded on capital markets.

EVA™ is a Stern Stewart registered trademark.

The alternative golden rule of value creation for a profit centre is:

EVA > 0

You now have two very powerful tools to assess the performance of each profit centre, RAROC or EVA. The two measures are related as both include the allocated profit and the allocated equity. In recent years, many banks have adopted the economic profit or EVA approach as it takes explicitly into account the size of the business unit and its cost of equity. It allows the actual amount of value created by a business unit over a specific time period to be calculated. With this focus on value-based management, profit centres are increasingly called value centres (VCs).

As the manager of a profit centre, you would prefer to receive a very low equity allocation in order to improve your RAROC or EVA. The fair allocation of profit and equity to a particular profit centre is a major issue, which will be discussed in the following stages.

KEY POINTS

➡ Two measures of a profit centre's performance have been developed:

➡ RAROC = allocated profit after tax/allocated equity.

➡ Golden rule for value creation: RAROC > cost of equity.

➡ EVA = allocated profit after tax − (allocated equity ¥ cost of equity).

➡ Golden rule for value creation: EVA > 0.

EXERCISE **STAGE FOUR**

The allocated profit after tax of the corporate banking division is $4 million. An equity of $20 million has been allocated to this profit centre.

Compute the RAROC, the cost of equity and the EVA knowing that the risk-free rate on government bonds is 10% and that the market demands a risk premium of 5% on bank shares.

Please calculate:

RAROC $= \dfrac{\ldots\ldots}{\ldots\ldots} =$

Cost of equity $= \ldots\ldots + \ldots\ldots =$

EVA $= \ldots\ldots - (\ldots\ldots \times \ldots\ldots) =$

Golden rule for value creation:

Value is created by the corporate banking unit whenever the RAROC of …….. exceeds the cost of equity of ………., or when the EVA of ……… million is positive.

PROFIT ALLOCATION AND TRANSFER PRICING FOR DEPOSITS AND LOANS

In Stage 4, we introduced the EVA measure to evaluate the performance of individual business units.

As the new CFO, you want to know which business units create value for shareholders, and which ones require intensive care.

Your priority is to evaluate the performance of branches that collect deposits from the public and make loans. You ask the head of Accounting and Control to compute the profitability of deposits and loans.

Profitability of deposits and loans: the need for a relevant transfer price

Let us consider the balance sheet introduced in Stage 1.

Balance sheet (31 December 2000)

Assets		Liabilities and shareholders' equity	
Reserves with central bank	40	Demand deposits	500
Consumer loans	300	Term deposits	300
Corporate loans	200		
Interbank loans	300	Interbank deposits	200
Government bonds	230	Equity	100
Fixed assets	30		
Total	1100	Total	1100

Deposits and loans are collected by various branches located in several towns. Let us consider the branch located in central Paris. Here is its balance sheet.

Assets ($million)		Liabilities ($million)	
Consumer loans	60	Term deposits	70
Corporate loans	40		
Fixed assets	10		
Total	110	Total	70

You will notice that the balance sheet of a specific branch does not need to balance as the granting of loans could exceed the collection of deposits (as in the case of our branch) or vice versa. Let us measure the performance of this branch.

The case of deposits

We shall first compute *the profitability on the term deposits of $300 million collected from the public*. Straight accounting leads to:

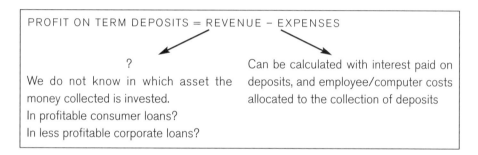

PROFIT ON TERM DEPOSITS = REVENUE – EXPENSES

?
We do not know in which asset the money collected is invested. In profitable consumer loans? In less profitable corporate loans?

Can be calculated with interest paid on deposits, and employee/computer costs allocated to the collection of deposits

To be able to compute the profitability of term deposits, we need to specify the relevant *revenue* that should be attributed to the term deposits.

Consider the following question: e-Bank has collected in total $300 million in term deposits. What would the bank do if it collected $330 million instead of $300 million, or if it collected only $270 million instead of $300 million?

Term deposit: 300

330 {
In most countries, the additional cash of $30 million will go to the bank's treasury and will be invested in interbank loans or will be used to reduce interbank deposits.

270 {
The bank is short of cash. e-Bank's treasury will finance this deficit by increasing interbank deposits or reducing interbank assets.

27

Therefore the interbank position acts as a liquidity cushion (expanding when additional deposits are collected, or shrinking when deposits are lost).

As we mentioned in Stage 1, the rate applied to interbank business is the interbank rate, often referred to as the market rate.

Since a change in deposits will affect the interbank[1] position of e-Bank, we want to ensure that the manager of the branch in central Paris takes this into account, and the revenue (the transfer price) allocated to deposit collection will be the interbank rate (the market rate).

The case of loans

Just as you did for deposits, you want to measure the profitability of the consumer loans granted by the branch. According to standard accounting:

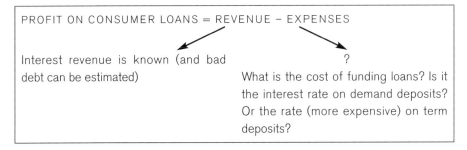

PROFIT ON CONSUMER LOANS = REVENUE − EXPENSES

Interest revenue is known (and bad debt can be estimated)

?

What is the cost of funding loans? Is it the interest rate on demand deposits? Or the rate (more expensive) on term deposits?

In the case of loans, the revenue is known but the funding cost needs to be estimated. Again, we will focus on the impact on e-bank's balance sheet of expanding or reducing the loan portfolio.

As with deposits, changes in the loan portfolios are managed through the interbank position. An increase in loans will be funded by a decrease in the interbank position, while a decrease in loans will imply an increase in the interbank position.

If a change in the volume of loans has an impact on the interbank position, the loan manager should receive the right signal. As with deposits, the transfer price for loans will be the interbank rate.

Which maturity?

An additional issue concerns the appropriate maturity of the transfer price. As we observe several interbank rates, the one month-to-maturity rate, the two month-to maturity rate, etc., we need to select a specific rate. A very simple rule is applied: the Matching Maturity Rule.

---

[1] This story is relevant in many countries with fairly liquid interbank or bond markets. Whenever this is not the case, one should always ask the simple question: if customers' deposits increase or decrease, what is the impact on the bank's balance sheet? An answer to that question will guide the choice of the relevant transfer price.

For example, we will use a one-year interbank rate to remunerate a one-year deposit and a two-years-to-maturity interbank rate as the cost of funding a two-years-to-maturity loan. Not only does this principle seem completely intuitive, it will also protect the branch manager against interest rate fluctuation.[2]

EXAMPLE

When you collect a one-year-to-maturity deposit, ALM will give you as transfer price (revenue) a one-year-to-maturity market rate.

When you make a loan of two-years-to-maturity, ALM will give you a fixed two-year cost of fund.

The interest margin that the branch earns on these deposits and loans is therefore locked in, fully protected against future interest rate fluctuation.

The matched maturity interbank rate is also called the matched maturity marginal value of fund (MMMVF).

Transfer price = matched maturity interbank rate = MMMVF.

 ## ASK/BID RATE and RESERVE REQUIREMENT

In Stage 1, we introduced two interbank rates: the ask rate on interbank assets and the bid rate on interbank deposits. In addition, we mentioned the reserve requirement regulation.

When it comes to the management of the interbank position, one does not always know which side of the balance sheet (assets or deposits) will be affected by the collection of deposits. Therefore, very often the average of the ask and bid interbank rates is used as the transfer price.

As far as the central bank's regulation is concerned, the reserve requirement implies that part of the deposits collected will not be available for investment purposes, but will have to be kept at the central bank. This costly regulation has to be taken into account to calculate the relevant transfer price (see the Note for the computation of a transfer price integrating the reserve requirement).

---

[2] See what would happen if maturity matching was not used. If a one-year-to-maturity fixed-rate deposit were collected, and a one-month interbank rate used as a transfer price, the profitability of that account would go up and down with the level of the one-month rate. To protect the manager against interest rate fluctuation, a matched-maturity market rate is used. Of course, for the bank as a whole, the maturity of deposits is unlikely to match the maturity of loans, but this mismatch will be managed by the ALM group.

Imagine that the term deposits[1] collected by the branch in central Paris (70) have a maturity of one year, that the three month-to-maturity interbank rate is 5%, that the one-year-to-maturity interbank rate is 6%, and that the bank pays 4% on deposits. The interest margin on the deposits will be calculated as follows:

Interest margin on deposits = (6% × 70) – (4% × 70) = 1.4

A very similar reasoning will apply to the evaluation of the interest margin on loans.

Imagine that the maturity of consumer and corporate loans is one and two years respectively, that the one-year and two-year-maturity interbank rates are respectively 6% and 7%, and that you charge 10% on consumer loans and 7.5% on corporate loans. The interest margin on loans for the branch in central Paris is calculated as follows:

Interest margin = margin on consumer loans + margin on corporate loans
= [(10% – 6%) x 60] + [(7.5 % – 7%) x 40] = 2.6

The net interest margin on deposits and loans for the branch is:

Total net interest margin = margin on deposits + margin on loans
= 1.4 + 2.6 = 4

 **Managerial rule**

A managerial rule follows from the choice of the transfer price:

> The main objective in collecting deposits and making loans is to increase the net interest margin. Each margin is calculated vis-à-vis the matched-maturity marginal value of fund.

The logic of transfer pricing for deposits and loans can be visualized as shown in Figure 5.1.

It is as if the deposits collected by the branches were transferred to e-Bank's treasury, the branches receiving as income the MMMVF. It is as if the loans granted by the branches were funded with money lent by the treasury at the MMMVF.

As branch managers collect deposits and grant loans to increase their net interest margin, it can often happen that the maturities of deposits and

---

[1] With no reserve requirement.

Figure 5.1 Transfer pricing for deposits and loans

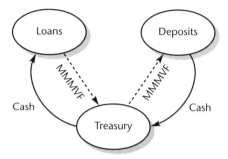

loans are different. It will be the responsibility of the treasury to manage the maturity mismatch created by commercial branches. The management of interest rate and liquidity risks is discussed in Stages 11 and 15.

KEY POINTS

➡ The transfer price for deposits and loans is the matched-maturity interbank rate (or the matched-maturity marginal value of fund, MMMVF).

➡ Deposits and lending units will attempt to increase the net interest margin on deposits and loans.

➡ The net interest margin of a branch is the sum of the margin on deposits and the margin on loans.

Note: reserve requirement and transfer price

Let us assume that:

D	= Deposits
d	= Deposit rate
r	= Central bank reserve requirement (in percentage of deposits)
R	= Reserves with the central bank ($R = r \times D$)
IA	= Interbank assets
i	= Interbank rate

Then we have:

Central bank reserves + interbank assets = deposits

Interest margin = revenue − expenses

$R + IA = D$
$IA = D − R$

$$\begin{aligned}
\text{Interest margin} &= (i \times IA) - (d \times D) = b \times (D{-}R) - (d \times D) \\
&= [i \times (D - r \times D)] - (d \times D) \\
&= i \times (1 - r) \times D - (d \times D)
\end{aligned}$$

The transfer price is the matched-maturity interbank rate adjusted by the central bank's reserve requirement $(i \times (1 − r))$.

EXERCISE STAGE FIVE

Here is the balance sheet of a bank branch located in Nice on the French Riviera. Taking into account that the reserve requirement of the central bank is 10% (no revenue paid on these reserves that must be held at the central bank), calculate the net interest margin on deposits, the net interest margin on loans, and the total net interest margin earned by this branch.

Asset		Liabilities	
Reserves (@10%):	30	Deposits (one year, rate = 1.7%):	100
Loans (three year, rate = 6%)):	200	Deposits (two year, rate = 2.15%):	200
Loans (five year, rate = 8%)):	300		

The interbank curve is as follows:

6-month rate:	2%
1-year rate:	3%
2-year rate:	3.5%
3-year rate:	4%
4-year rate:	4.5%
5-year rate:	5%

Net interest margin on deposits

Net interest margin on deposits of 100 = (..... − .....) × ..... = ...

Net interest margin on deposits of 200 = (..... − .....) × ..... = ...

Total net interest margin on deposits = ... + ... = ...

Net interest margin on loans

Net interest margin on loans of 200 = (..... − .....) × ..... = ...

Net interest margin on loans of 300 = (..... − .....) × ..... = ...

Total net interest margin on loans = ... + ... = ...

Total net interest margin = margin on deposits + margin on loans

= ..... + ... = ...

33

THE CAPITAL ADEQUACY
REGULATION

You found out in Stage 3 that one of the drivers of the return on equity was the leverage factor, that is the ratio debt/equity.

As one could be tempted to increase leverage (that is reduce equity and increase debt) to boost the reported ROE, central banks have devised international capital adequacy regulations.

As the new CFO, you must ensure that e-Bank meets this capital regulation at all times.

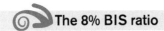 ## The 8% BIS ratio

History

One of the traditional missions of central banks is to ensure financial stability and solvency of the banking system. To achieve this objective, each national central bank forces banks to have a minimum level of equity to absorb losses in case of a recession.

However, if a central bank happens to be too severe with its capital requirement, banks could be tempted to migrate to a more lenient country with accommodating regulation. In order to prevent this kind of competition between countries, central bankers, who meet every month at the Bank for International Settlements (BIS) in Basle (Switzerland), have created a committee, the Basle Committee on Banking Supervision,[1] which aims to design a minimal equity regulation that all international banks should meet.

---

[1] The committee is made up of senior representatives of bank supervisory authorities and central banks from Belgium, Canada, France, Germany, Italy, Japan, Luxembourg, the Netherlands, Sweden, Switzerland, the United Kingdom and the United States.

The capital adequacy regulation

This regulation on equity is commonly referred to as the 'capital adequacy ratio', the 'BIS ratio' or the 'Cooke' ratio, after the UK's Peter Cooke who was the first chairman of the Basle Committee. This regulation, applied since January 1993, states that the capital ratio must exceed 8%. It has had a major impact around the world as the International Monetary Fund (IMF) and the World Bank enforce this ratio in a large number of countries.

BIS rule: (capital/weighted assets) ≥ 8%

BIS capital

As banks were concerned with their leverage driver, they lobbied very hard to have a measure of capital that would not include too much equity. In 1988, the negotiation came to an end with a measure of capital composed of two parts: Tier 1 (at least 4%) and Tier 2.

CAPITAL

TIER 1 is essentially made up of the equity reported in the balance sheet:

- Paid in capital.
- Retained earnings.
- General (disclosed) provisions: created to cover as yet unidentified risks.

TIER 2 includes additional elements such as:

- re-evaluation of premises (when real estate value changes);
- hidden reserves (which appear when excessive bad debt provisions on specific loans exist);
- 45% of unrealized gains on securities (when the market value of financial assets is different from the one reported in the book);
- subordinated debt (capped at 50% of Tier 1. It protects depositors who are paid before subordinated debt-holders in case of default of the bank).

The Basle Committee has imposed a minimum capital requirement that must be met by international banks. Each national central bank can adopt a more stringent regulation. On strict legal grounds, the Basle Committee has no authority to enforce the capital regulation, but its moral authority is such that no central bank would dare to adopt a more lenient capital regulation.

Assets weighing

In the measurement of the asset base, the regulators decided in 1988 to take into account credit risk. Assets on the balance sheet together with bank commitments (the off-balance sheet transactions) are weighted by a factor indicative of their credit risk (going from 0% for non-risky OECD public debt to 100% for risky private debts).

Weighing rules for assets are shown in Figure 6.1.

Figure 6.1 Weighing rules for assets

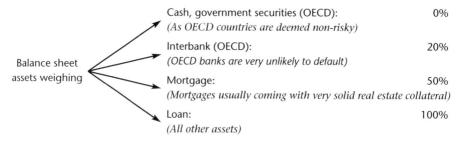

Balance sheet assets weighing

Cash, government securities (OECD):   0%
(As OECD countries are deemed non-risky)

Interbank (OECD):   20%
(OECD banks are very unlikely to default)

Mortgage: 50%
(Mortgages usually coming with very solid real estate collateral)

Loan: 100%
(All other assets)

(Weighing for the off-balance sheet items is given in the Note).

EXAMPLE

Let us take as an example the (slightly modified) e-Bank balance sheet.

Assets		Liabilities and shareholders' equity	
Reserves with central bank	40	Demand deposits	500
Mortgage loans	350	Term deposits	300
Corporate loans	300	Interbank deposits	240
Interbank loans	250	Subordinated debt	20
Government bonds	130	Equity	40
Fixed assets	30		
Total	1100	Total	1100

The risk-weighted assets (RWA) are calculated as follows:

RWA = 0% × (40 + 130) + 20% × (250) + 50% × (350) + 100% × (300 + 30) = 555

Tier 1 capital: 40/555 = 7.2%

Tier 2 capital: 20/555 = 3.6%

BIS capital ratio = Tier 1 + Tier 2 = 7.2% + 3.6% = 10.8%

> **KEY POINTS**
>
> ➡ Banks must obey the Basle Committee's regulation on bank capital, which calls for an 8% capital requirement on risk-adjusted assets.
>
> ➡ BIS ratio = capital adequacy ratio = Cooke ratio
>
> = (capital/weighed asset) ≥ 8%
>
> ➡ The capital (defined by the BIS) consists of two parts: Tier 1 (core capital) and Tier 2 (supplementary capital).
>
> Risk adjustment factors applying to positions (on and off-balance sheet) range from 0% to 100%.

As discussed in Stage 1, some banking transactions are off-balance sheet because, at origination, it does not affect the asset or debt. Two major categories are the guarantees and the derivative contracts.

Weighing system for off-balance sheet items

Guarantees are simply weighted by a credit conversion factor to measure the bank's loss if the guarantee was called in.

Guarantees	Credit conversion factor
1. Direct credit substitutes (standby letters of credit)	100%
2. Short-term self-liquidating trade-related contingency	20%
3. Asset sale with recourse	100%
4. Note issuance facilities (NIF)	50%

Derivatives: Forex, interest rate, equity, commodities

Derivatives such as forwards, futures or options are discussed in Stages 13 and 16. The credit risk is the potential cost of the contract when the counterparty defaults.

39

Current exposure method

Credit risk: replacement cost ('marking to market') + potential future credit exposure (add-on).

Residual maturity	Interest rate	Forex + Gold	Equity
Less than one year	Nil	1%	6%
One year to 5 years	0.5%	5%	8%
Over five years	1.5%	7.5%	10%

EXERCISE STAGE SIX

Here is the balance sheet of a bank. Compute the Tier 1 capital ratio, the Tier 2 ratio, and the overall BIS capital ratio.

Assets		Liabilities and shareholders' equity	
Reserves with central bank	60	Demand deposits	750
Mortgage loans	525	Term deposits	450
Corporate loans	450	Interbank deposits	370
Interbank loans	375	Subordinated debt	25
Government bonds	195	Equity	55
Fixed assets	45		
Total	1650	Total	1650

The risk-weighted assets would be calculated as follows:

RWA = 0% × (..... + ...) + 20% × (.....) + 50% × (.....)
  + 100% × (..... + ...) = ...s

Tier 1 capital: ..... / ..... = ... %

Tier 2 capital: ..... / ..... = ... %

BIS capital ratio = Tier 1 + Tier 2 = ... % + ... % = ... %

LOAN PRICING (1): THE 'EQUITY' SPREAD

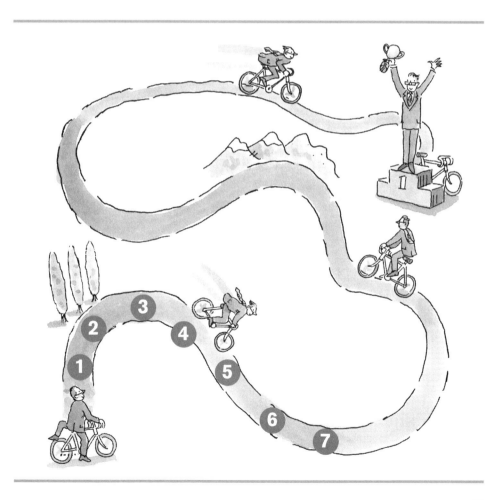

In Stage 6 we discussed how the BIS capital adequacy regulation is forcing banks to fund loans with equity. This raises immediately a question about the interest margin on loans needed to satisfy shareholders.

Your general manager has asked you to evaluate the impact of the 8% BIS ratio on loan pricing.

Break-even loan pricing and the 'equity' spread

Let us consider a loan of 100 that has a maturity of one year. The loan is funded partly on the interbank market and 8% capital.

Here is the funding structure:

Funding

Loan	100	Interbank deposit	92
		Equity	8

To keep the example simple, we have used 8 of equity even if the BIS definition of capital would have allowed us to use less equity (Tier 1) and more subordinated debt (Tier 2). Note also that the relevant debt is the interbank debt, not the deposits collected from customers. Indeed, according to Stage 5, we want to take into account the incremental impact of a loan on the interbank position of e-Bank.

The interbank rate is 10%, e-Bank pays a corporate tax rate of 40%, and the shareholders of e-Bank demand a minimum return (cost of equity) of 15%.

As your objective is value creation, you know that you must apply the fundamental managerial rule:

Market value > equity invested by shareholders.

In the context of lending and in order to know what is an acceptable loan rate for your shareholders, you will calculate the break-even loan rate, that is the rate at which there is a value creation of zero. Zero value creation means that the equity invested by shareholders (8) is just equal to the discounted value of future after-tax cash flows. With a value creation of zero, shareholders are indifferent about the bank making the loan or making an investment by themselves.

Equity invested = discounted value of the cash flows on the loan

After-tax cash flow of the loan

$$8 = \frac{\overbrace{\{(1 - 40\%) \times [(R \times 100) - (10\% \times 92)]\} + 100 - 92}}{1.15}$$

R = interest rate on loan
R × 100 = revenue on loan
10% = interbank rate
8 = equity; 92 = debt
10% × 92 = interest expense
15% = cost of equity
40% = tax rate

By solving this equation, you calculate a break-even interest rate R equal to 11.2%.

The break-even rate R of 11.2% implies that the present value of the loan transaction is exactly equal to 8, that is the equity invested by shareholders. There is no value creation in this case.

When you compare the break-even rate of 11.2% with the interbank rate of 10%, you obtain a break-even margin on this loan equal to: 11.2% – 10% = 1.2%

Break-even margin = break-even rate – interbank rate

You will notice that we did not include in the after-tax cash flows the operating expenses (employee or computer time) nor any cost for bad debt.

These elements will be considered separately in the next stage. We refer to the spread of 1.2% as the 'equity' spread. It is the interest margin on a loan necessary to satisfy shareholders.

'Equity' spread = break-even margin
= margin on loan necessary to satisfy shareholders

If there were no capital requirement, there would be no need for an 'equity' spread. In other words, as soon as equity is used to finance a loan, profit has to be made in order to satisfy shareholders' expectations. The 'equity spread' is the first component of a margin on a loan. Other components discussed at a later stage will include credit risk and operating expenses.

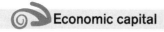 **Economic capital**

The above loan pricing example has shown that a margin of 1.2% was necessary to offer an acceptable return to shareholders. But any corporate banker working in an international environment will tell you that intense competition between banks has driven margins down to 20 basis points (0.2%) in some countries.

Given the need to satisfy shareholders, banks have analyzed the strategic implications of the BIS 8% capital regulation. Three comments are frequently heard.

1. The above analysis is not comprehensive because the loan pricing example took into account only the loan transaction. Quite often, banks will be selling additional services (cash management, foreign exchange, etc.) so that the margin could be lower if other sources of revenue existed. Those bankers argue correctly that it is the overall customer relationships (all sources of revenue included) that matter. Indeed, one could lend below break-even 'equity' spread to attract a profitable customer.

2. In order to avoid this costly capital regulation, bankers sell loans to third parties. As the sale of a loan takes it away from the bank's balance sheet, there is no more capital requirement and need for an 'equity' spread. In Stage 9, we will discuss the process of securitization that is the sale and conversion of loans into securities.

3. Last but not least, banks have realized that the 8% BIS ratio was the result of a diplomatic agreement, a compromise among central bankers. Instead of allocating the same 8% to all loans, specialists suggest allocating 'economic capital'. Safe loans would command a small capital allocation, while risky loans would command a larger amount of capital.

Before we discuss the economic capital allocation process, let us first analyze its strategic importance. In Table 7.1, we use the same loan pricing example as above and calculate the 'equity' spread for several equity allocations ranging from 1% to 12%, and for different tax rates ranging from 0% to 40%. For instance, the case discussed above of 8% equity with a tax rate of 40% leads to the necessary 'equity' spread of 1.2%.

Table 7.1 Loan equity spreads (%)

Equity alloc. Tax rate	(Cost of debt: 10%; cost of equity: 15%)					
	1%	4%	6%	8%	10%	12%
0%	0.05	0.2	0.3	0.4	0.5	0.6
20%	0.09	0.35	0.53	0.7	0.88	1.05
30%	0.11	0.46	0.69	0.91	1.14	1.37
40%	0.15	0.6	0.9	1.2	1.5	1.8

If you can convince your chief financial officer that the risk of the loan is low and that 1% of economic capital is needed, you will notice that the required 'equity' spread goes down to 15 basis points (0.15%). Very good news! But it raises immediately the following question: How is the economic capital allocated?

Economic capital allocation

The allocation of economic capital is based on the observation that the equity of any company is a buffer whose role is to absorb eventual losses to avoid bankruptcy. Indeed, losses reduce retained earnings and the equity base. When the equity is depleted, there is a risk of default.

So, if you consider the curve in Figure 7.1 that describes the probability distribution of the income on a loan, the risk for e-Bank is related to losses on the loan, the downside risk on the left side of the curve. Equity is needed to cover the downside risk. In theory, one would need a very large amount of equity to cover all possible shortfalls. As this would be too expensive, banks use a pragmatic approach whereby the equity allocated must cover *most* of the loan losses (for instance 99%).

Figure 7.1 Probability distribution of income on a loan[1]

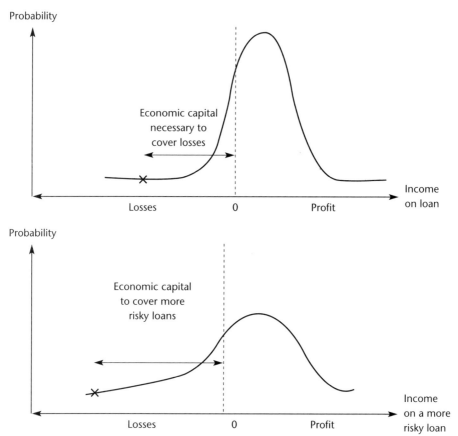

Since economic capital is the capital necessary to cover potential losses, it is often referred to as risk-based capital.

In recent years, many banks around the world have moved to an economic capital allocation in order to have a better understanding of risk and better pricing of loans. However, this creates a problem as central banks continue to require the standard 8% BIS ratio, applying the same weight to all loans.

The discrepancy between *regulatory* capital and *economic* capital explains why a large number of banks are lobbying for a revision of the international capital adequacy regulation.

---

[1] Historical data on loans of a specific risk category could help to calculate the probability distribution. Alternative approaches are based on the volatility of the value of equity and assets of a company.

A new BIS regulation for the new millennium?

The Basle Committee on Banking Supervision and the banking community are negotiating a new agreement, referred to as Basle II, that would demand less capital for safe loans and more capital for risky loans. The aim is to bring the BIS capital guidelines in line with the economic capital allocation of banks. This would make life much easier for banks as economic capital would be closer to regulatory capital. The outcome of this negotiation is expected in 2002, with eventual application in 2005.

KEY POINTS

➡ The break-even rate on a loan is the rate at which there is no value creation.

➡ 'Equity' spread: margin on loan necessary to reward shareholders.

➡ Economic capital is the capital necessary to cover the potential losses on the loan (also referred to as the risk-based capital).

➡ Economic capital allocation allows banks to have a better understanding of risk and better loan pricing rules.

49

EXERCISE STAGE SEVEN

Compute the break-even loan rate and the 'equity' spread on a one-year-to-maturity loan of $100. The loan is funded with 95 of interbank debt and 5 of equity. The interbank rate is 10%, the corporate tax rate is 30% and the cost of equity is 15%.

Hint: equity invested = present value of loan transaction.

LOAN PRICING (2): CREDIT RISK AND CREDIT PROVISIONS

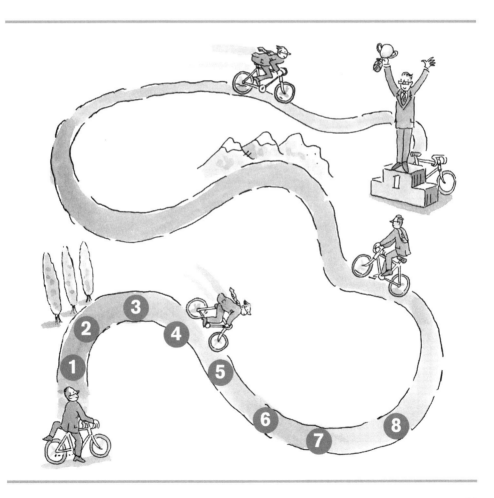

As Stage 8 is more sophisticated, the reader can skip it without any loss of continuity.

In Stage 7, we learned that equity funding creates a need for an 'equity' spread to satisfy shareholders.

In Stage 8, we shall introduce credit risk and loan losses explicitly.

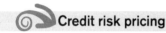

Credit risk pricing

Let us consider the following loan proposal:

Funding			
Loan	100	Interbank debt	94
		Equity	6

- $100 million two-year-to-maturity fixed-rate loan (interest paid at the end of the year and principal at maturity).
- Corporate tax rate: 40%.
- Shareholders' opportunity return (cost of equity): 13.2%.
- Fixed interbank rate: 10% for the first year and 10% for the second year.
- Equity funding (economic capital): 6%.
- Interbank funding: 94%.
- Probability of default in Year One: 0%.
- Probability of default in Year Two: 3%.
- Recovery of 60 in case of default (or loss given default = 40).

As we learned in Stage 7 (loan pricing), the break-even loan interest rate R is such that the discounted value of expected after-tax cash flows is equal to the initial equity investment (6). In this two-year-to-maturity loan example, the calculation is as follows:

Present value of cash flow
received the first year

$$\text{Equity} = 6 = \frac{((R \times 100) - (94 \times 0.10)) \times (1 - 0.4)}{1.132} +$$

Present value of expected cash flow received
in Year Two if borrower is solvent or not

| In case of no default | In case of default | Cost of funding in Year Two |

$$\frac{0.97 \times ((1 - 04) \times R \times 100 + 100) + 0.03 \times (60 + (0.4 \times 40))}{1.132^2} - \frac{94 \times 0.10 \times (1 - 0.4) + 94}{1.132^2}$$

Solving this relation leads to the break-even loan rate = 11.45%.

Note that the break-even interest rate takes into account three factors: the amount of equity funding, the probability of default, and the recovery rate in case of default. The expected cash flow in Year Two demands some clarification. There is 97% probability of being repaid and 3% probability of a borrower's default. In that case, the bank recovers 60 and has a tax shield on the loss of 40 (40% × 40). The tax shield (a tax reduction) arises because the loss will reduce taxable profit so that less tax is being paid.

A bank pricing its loan at the break-even rate will ensure that the value of the transaction is equal to the equity invested. There would be no value creation in that case. As we discussed in Stage 7, a bank can decide to price its loan below the break-even rate if additional revenues from selling services (such as foreign exchange or cash management) provide an additional source of revenue.

An issue closely related to loan pricing from a methodology viewpoint is the creation of credit risk provisions.[1] For instance, imagine that the loan is priced at 11.45%. At the end of the first year when the interest rate on the loan is paid, should e-Bank recognize the interest received as a full income, or should the bank create a credit risk provision for potential future losses? This issue is of great importance as it will affect the *risk-adjusted performance* of a loan department.

---

[1] Credit risk provisions are also called provisions for bad debt, or provisions for doubtful loans.

Measuring credit risk provisions: 'lend now, lose later'

The early provisioning of loans is of great practical importance. If the interest income earned on the loan at the end of the first year were considered as profit, there would be great incentives for lenders to make high-margin (and often high-risk) loans with a long maturity with the objective of showing very strong profit in the early years. If this lending strategy would be good for the performance and the bonus of the loan manager at the end of the year, it could hurt the bank in the future when loan losses show up. To reduce the incentive for high-margin/high-risk lending, banks need imperatively to create *early* provisions.

To calculate fair credit risk provisions, we simply observe that, after the first year, the bank has received the interest margin after tax and has in its portfolio a loan and a debt with a maturity of one year. So, the profit of a loan department should include the net interest margin received plus any change in the net value of the loan (loan minus debt).

All the above assumptions being unchanged, the net value of the loan at the end of Year One is calculated as follows:

$$\textit{Net loan value} = \frac{0.97 \times [100 + (11.45) \times (1 - 0.4)] + 0.03 \times [60 + (0.4 \times 40)]}{1.132}$$

$$- \frac{[(94 \times 0.1 \times (1 - 0.4)) + 94]}{1.132} = 93.59 - 88.02 = 5.57$$

The net loan value was 6 at the beginning of the year. As it is now valued at 5.57, there has been a loss of value of 0.43 during the year, and the profit of the loan should be measured as follows:

Profit on the loan = interest margin after tax + change in value

$$= (1 - 0.4) \times [(11.45\% \times 100) - (10\% \times 94)] + (5.57 - 6) = 1.23 - 0.43 = 0.8[2]$$

Although the interest has been paid by the borrower, there is already the need to create a provision at the end of Year One. This early provision is referred to in some banks as 'ex ante' provision as no problem has yet been identified.[3] In our example in which bankruptcy can happen only in the second year, the

---

[2] You will notice that the profit (0.8) divided by equity (6) is equal to 13.2%, the return demanded by the shareholders. This is expected as the break-even interest rate of 11.45% was chosen to give the minimum return demanded by shareholders.

[3] The approach used to calculate the provisions is based on standard finance present value. It is fully consistent with the accounting rules calling for fair value accounting.

break-even rate of 11.45% is necessary to cover the potential risk of default in Year Two. This is the reason why we need to put some revenue aside (credit risk provision) to cover potential future losses. Remember that if no early provisions were being created, there would be too much incentive to go into high-margin/high-risk lending in order to show good early profit.

KEY POINTS

➡ The interest margin on a loan should include three components:

   ■ an 'equity' spread to reward shareholders;

   ■ a 'credit risk' spread to cover expected losses;

   ■ a spread to cover operating expenses (such as wages).

➡ Any bank needs to define very early fair credit risk provisions (interest earned in the early life of a loan is not to be considered as full income).

➡ If no provisions were created, there would be too much incentive to go into high-margin/high-risk lending in order to show good early profit.

➡ Profit on a loan = interest margin after tax + change in net loan value.

EXERCISE STAGE EIGHT

This exercise concerns a two-year-to-maturity loan. It has two parts:

- today, the issue is to decide whether a loan proposal creates value for the bank;

- a year later, an interest margin has been earned and the question is how much profit to accrue to the loan department.

Part one – today

Should the bank approve the following loan proposal with a loan rate of 14%? In other words, does the loan proposal create value for the bank?

Loan proposal

- Two-year-to-maturity loan of 100, with interest paid every year and principal of 100 at maturity.

- Equity (economic capital) funding = 6.

- Cost of equity = 15%.

- Probability of default in Year One: 0%.

- Probability of default in Year Two: 4%.

- Recovery in case of default: 20 (or loss given default: 80).

- Interbank funding: 94 (cost of debt = 10%).

- Corporate tax rate = 25%.

- Loan rate = R = 14%.

Given the data above, should you accept the loan proposal?

Reminder: a loan creates value when the equity invested in the transaction is smaller than the present value of expected cash flows.

You have first to compute the expected cash flows for Years One and Two, discounted at the cost of equity:

$$\textbf{Equity} = 6 = \frac{\textbf{((revenue – cost)} \times \textbf{(tax factor))}}{\textbf{(1 + cost of equity)}} \textbf{in Year 1}$$

$$+ \frac{\textbf{((revenue – cost in case of default and no default)} \times \textbf{(tax factor))}}{\textbf{(1 + cost of equity)}^2} \textbf{in Year 2}$$

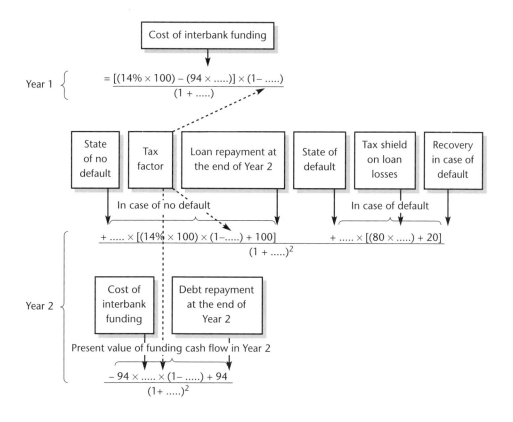

Part two – at end of Year One

- $ million 100 two-year-to-maturity fixed-rate loan (interest, 14, paid at end of the year and principal at maturity).
- Corporate tax rate: 25%.
- Shareholders' opportunity return =15% (cost of equity).
- Equity funding: 6%.
- Interbank funding: 94% (cost of debt: 10%).

- Probability of default in Year Two: 4%.
- Recovery of 20 in case of default or loss given default: 80.

At the end of the first year, the loan department has received an interest margin on the loan and has a loan and a debt with one more year to maturity. Let us first compute the net loan value, that is the value of the loan net of the value of the debt:

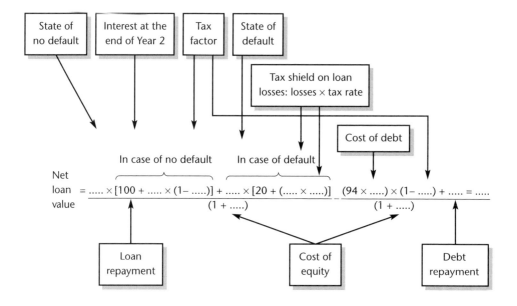

Once you get the net loan value, you can compute the total profit on the loan:

Profit on the loan = interest margin after tax + change in net loan value

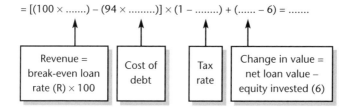

SECURITIZATION

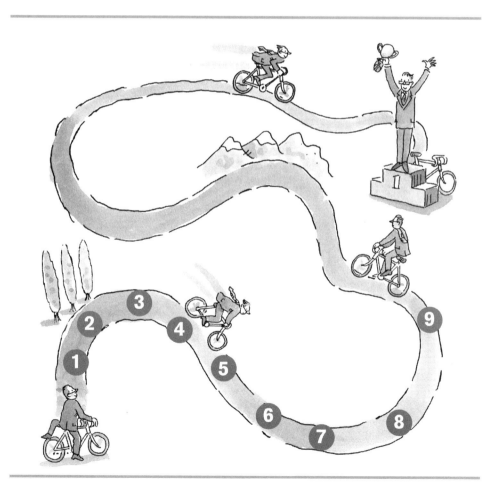

In recent years, banks have developed techniques to sell loans to investors. This mechanism is called 'securitization'.

As we observed in Stage 7, one of the economic motives for this process is to avoid the costly BIS capital regulation.

 ## The securitization process

Securitization involves the sale of loans to investors. These may be individuals or institutional investors such as pensions funds, life insurance companies or other banks.

As a potential investor, your uncle is very worried about the quality of the loan sold by e-Bank. So, to reassure him, you explain to him that two additional parties are involved in securitization: a credit risk insurer and a rating agency. The general mechanism of securitization is given in Figure 9.1.

The sale of loans to investors is made through a special corporate entity called a special purpose vehicle (SPV). The SPV buys the loan from e-Bank, and in order to finance this acquisition, it issues securities (shares) which are sold to investors.

Usually, the originating bank continues to service the loan (for a fee) and the net cash flows generated on the loan are passed to investors through the SPV.

Often, to reassure the investors:

- a third party steps in promising to guarantee part or all the credit risk on the loans. As an example, re-insurance companies have recently offered their services to guarantee credit risk;
- a rating agency analyzes the securitization structure and gives a high rating on the securities.

In many countries, laws have been passed to allow securitization of loans.

Figure 9.1 How securitization works

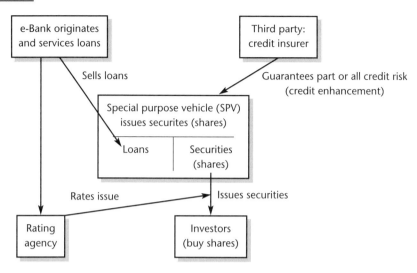

The economics of securitization

How can this rather complex transaction increase e-Bank's market value? What are the main economic advantages of securitization?

1. First you will notice that e-Bank keeps a part of the revenue. Indeed, a fee is retained for servicing the loan. Second, if the revenue on the loan is attractive, it can be sold to the SPV at a high price, creating a capital gain for e-Bank.

2. Banks have several good reasons for selling loans:

   - The most obvious one (if we refer to Stage 7) is to avoid the costly equity requirement. Once the loan is sold, the capital requirement has no more reason to be, and there is no more need for an 'equity' spread.[1]

   - Another reason is liquidity, that is when a bank needs cash to fund its portfolio. Securitization enables the bank to reach a new class of investors.

   - One additional incentive is diversification of credit risks when a bank has too large an exposure to a particular business sector.

---

[1] But the investor could demand an 'equity' spread if he/she needs equity to fund the loan.

KEY POINTS

➡ Securitization is a process that allows banks to sell loans to investors.

➡ There are different economic motives for selling loans:

■ avoid BIS capital requirement;

■ liquidity;

■ diversify credit risk.

A loan with a low credit risk and a book value of 100 has two years to maturity.

The expected cash flows generated are as follows:

Year Zero	Year One	Year Two
Loan = 100	+ 10	+ 110

Given that the expected return on corporate bonds with a similar level of risk is 8%, at what price should this securitized loan be sold to investors?

Compute the capital gain realized by the bank selling that loan.

VALUE CREATION: A SUMMARY

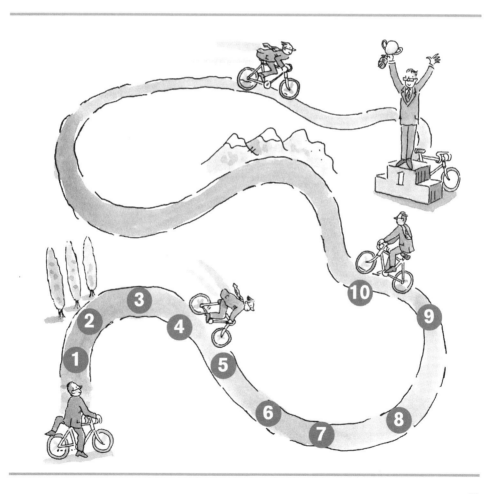

Congratulations! You have just completed the first part of the book. At this stage, you might want to sum up what you have learned regarding shareholder value creation. Remember that asset and liability management has two parts: value creation and risk management. We have reached the end of the first part.

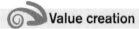

Value creation

There are three building blocks to remember. They concern value creation at the overall level of the bank, value creation at the level of a profit centre, and the implications for loan pricing, credit risk provisioning and securitization.

1 Overall bank level

As is the case for any corporation listed on a stock exchange, shareholders want to ensure that the value of their shares exceeds the amount of money invested in the company (the equity). Technically, this implies that the long-term return on equity should exceed the cost of equity demanded by the market. This cost is estimated by the opportunity return that is available to shareholders investing in other financial instruments.

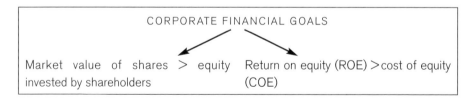

CORPORATE FINANCIAL GOALS

Market value of shares > equity invested by shareholders   Return on equity (ROE) > cost of equity (COE)

2 Profit centre level

The ROE objective is relevant for the corporation as a whole. However, to make it operational, banks are setting corporate goals for profit centres, such as economic value added or economic profit.

Economic value added = (profit allocated)
− (allocated equity × cost of equity) > 0

Three technical issues arise in the calculation.

1. Transfer price for deposits and loans: matched-maturity market rate. The bank must send the relevant signal to the managers collecting deposits or granting loans.

2. Equity allocation: regulatory capital versus economic (risk-based) capital. As a manager, you will prefer to receive a low equity allocation as your performance will look better. Banks are increasingly shifting away from the use of regulatory capital to an economic capital allocation based on the risk actually taken by a business unit. Risk represents the potential losses that could occur.

3. Provisions for credit risk. An important issue concerns the proper recognition of the potential losses arising in a transaction and the need to create provisions early.

3 Loan management

The corporate goal of value creation has direct implications for loan pricing and securitization.

- Break-even loan pricing: equity invested = present value of expected cash flows. We have seen that the margin on loans should incorporate three elements: an 'equity' spread to reward shareholders, the probability of default, and the amount that would be recovered in case of default.

- Securitization: should the bank keep or sell the loans? Incentives for selling loans include the freeing of the bank's equity, access to liquidity, or the diversification of the loan portfolio.

stage

THE CONTROL OF INTEREST RATE RISK (1): THE REPRICING GAPS

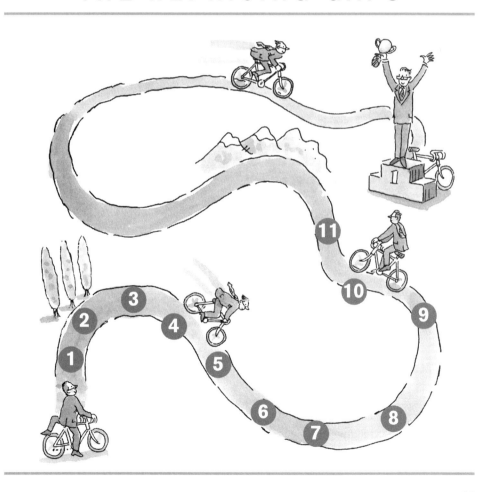

In Stage 5, we discussed transfer prices and the calculation of interest margins on deposits and loans. We mentioned that a problem could arise if the maturities of assets and deposits are not matched.

As interest rate fluctuations could affect the net interest margin of e-Bank, you need to understand how to measure and manage interest rate risk.

 Measuring interest rate risk

The impact of interest rate fluctuations on the profitability of e-Bank can be represented as shown in Figure 11.1.

The specialists in the bank provide an interest rate forecast (the expected interest rate) and the accounting department calculates the 'pro forma' profitability given that forecast. As a risk manager, you need to understand how the profit will be affected if the forecast is wrong. In Figure 11.1, profitability goes up when the interest rate increases, while profit goes down if the interest rate goes down. This is only an example, as the reverse could also occur. The purpose of interest rate risk management is to evaluate and manage the impact of interest rate fluctuation on profitability.

Figure 11.1 The impact of interest rate fluctuations on profitability

Interest rate risk is part of a larger group of risks called market risks. These include the potential losses arising from a movement of interest rates, exchange rates, equity prices and commodity prices. These risks arise when banks trade foreign currency-denominated assets, shares or commodities such as gold or silver.

However, before we can discuss the evaluation of interest rate risk, we must remember two major accounting rules for bank profit.

Bank accounting: accrual versus marked-to-market

Bank accountants separate transactions into two categories (Figure 11.2):

- the banking (or accrual) book;
- the trading book.

1. The key accounting characteristic of the banking book is that loans, deposits and bonds (investment portfolio[1]) are recorded at their historical cost (i.e. a loan of 1 million remains recorded at 1 million over the life of the loan). The key consequence for the profit and loss account is that the accrual book generates a net interest margin (NIM) which is the difference between the interest received and the interest paid. Since the net interest margin is usually a major component of a bank's P&L, the impact of interest rate risk on the NIM has to be analyzed very carefully.

2. The key accounting characteristic of the trading book is that it is marked-to-market every day. Marking-to-market means that the present value of the portfolio is calculated on a daily basis. When assets are traded, one uses the end-of-the-day market price. If an asset is not traded, its *fair* discounted value is calculated. As a consequence, the value of the trading book may vary from day to day, generating a change of value in the P&L.

Figure 11.2 **The two categories for bank accounting**

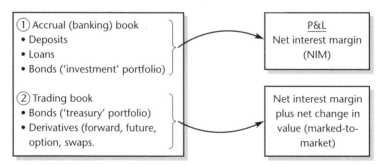

_____
[1] Bonds are recorded in the investment portfolio if the intent is to keep them for a long period (in some banks more than a year). Bonds are recorded in the treasury portfolio if the intent is to trade them frequently.

71

Diffcrent tools are used by banks to evaluate the interest rate risk on the banking and trading books. These include the repricing bucket, the simulation model and the economic value at risk (duration of equity). We will focus first on the banking book (repricing bucket and simulation tools).

The repricing bucket (gaps)

The first tool used by e-Bank to control its interest rate exposure on the banking book is the repricing bucket (also called 'repricing gap' or 'interest rate sensitivity' table). The repricing bucket provides information about the time of repricing of all assets and liabilities.

It allows a simple question to be answered: if interest rates go up (or down) tomorrow, when will the interest revenue or cost and the net interest margin be affected (Table 11.1)?

Let us start with the assets booked on the balance sheet at a specific date. If the interest rate level changes tomorrow, at what time in the future shall we be able to adjust the interest income on the asset?

Table 11.1 The effect of interest rate fluctuations

Repricing time in months	0–3	3–6	6–9	9–12	12–24	24–36	Non-interest rate sensitive
Assets							
Reserves with central bank							40
Mortgage loan	30	30	30	30	140	90	
Corporate loans	200	50	50				
Interbank assets	50	50	100	50			
Government bonds	10	10	10	10	45	45	
Fixed assets							30
Total	290	140	190	90	185	135	70
Liabilities and equity							
Demand deposits	500						
Term deposits		150	150				
Interbank deposits	100	140					
Subordinated debt					25		
Equity							35
Total	600	290	150		25		35
Gap	−310	−150	40	90	160	135	35
Cumulative gap	−310	−460	−420	−330	−170	−35	0

For short maturities or floating rate assets, the repricing will take place rapidly. For assets with a fixed interest, the repricing will be delayed until the maturity of that asset. For instance, in the case of e-Bank, we observe that a total asset of 290 would be repriced in the coming three months,[2] while another 140 could be repriced in the second quarter.

Next, let us take all the liabilities. If the interest rate level changes tomorrow, at what time shall we have to adjust the cost of deposits?

In the case of e-Bank, a total of 600 would be repriced in the coming three months, while another 290 would be repriced in the second quarter.

Then, we calculate the *gap*, that is the difference between assets and liabilities. For instance, a negative gap of –310 in the next 0–3-month time bucket indicates an excess of short-term deposits. The reading is that if the interest rate goes down, it is good for the bank, but if the interest rate goes up, it is bad news.

Finally, the *cumulative gap* is a means of evaluating the total net exposure over time. In the case of e-Bank, the first gap is –310, but due to a repricing of –150 in the second quarter, the total exposure for the second quarter is –460. If the interest rate goes up and remains high, the first gap of –310 indicates that the first quarter P&L will be affected by a repricing of a net –310, while the second-quarter P&L will be affected by a repricing of a net –460. A risk manager will have to ensure that each of these cumulative gaps is not too large.

Reading the repricing bucket

If the repricing gap provides some useful information on the mismatching of assets and liabilities, it does not yet offer a direct assessment of the interest rate risk faced by a bank.

What the ALCO wants to know is the effect of a change of interest rate, say 1%, on the net interest margin or the profit of the bank. If the interest rate changes, do we lose the entire earnings of the year or only a small part?

A very useful concept, the earnings-at-risk (EAR), will provide this information.

---

[2] The interval of three months is used for the sake of simplicity. Banks use shorter time intervals.

EXAMPLE

In the case of the first-quarter gap of −310, the impact of an increase of 1% on the net interest margin of the quarter will be measured as follows:[3]

$$\text{Earnings-at-risk (EAR)} = \frac{|(1\% \times 290) - (1\% \times 600)|}{4} = \frac{|- 310| \times 1\%}{4} = \frac{|-3.1|}{4} = 0.775$$

$$= |gap| \times \Delta \text{ rate}$$

The EAR is very useful to senior members of ALCO as it indicates the exposure of profit to interest rate change. In many banks, the board will put a limit on the maximum EAR.

Reporting risk

In the above example, a change of 1% was used to keep the mathematics simple, but in reality you should consider what could be a potential rate change: 1% or 5%? Obviously the earnings-at-risk would be much larger for a 5% rate change.

To answer this question about the relevant volatility of interest rates, the ALCO must first determine the following. If interest rates start to move in the wrong direction, the treasury will not stay idle and take the loss but will take action to close the gap. How much time will be needed to close the position: one day or one week? This time interval, referred to as the *holding* or *defeasance* period, is important as interest rates are not likely to move much over a very short period, but could move much more over a longer period. In any particular country, the size of the position and the liquidity of the markets would indicate how long it should take to close a position.

The practice is to report two types of information: a measure of risk under 'normal' times, and a measure of risk for 'stress' scenarios.

Earnings-at-risk in 'normal' times

In this measure of risk, you report the impact of a change of interest rate likely to cover most of the potential cases (for instance, 95% of the cases.[4] Historical data are usually used to analyze the 'normal' volatility in a specific country).

$$\text{EAR}_{95\%} = |gap| \times (\Delta_{95\%} \text{ rate})$$

---

[3] We divide by 4 to calculate a quarterly revenue.
[4] The confidence level of 95% is arbitrary. Some banks work with 97.5% while others use 99%.

If this '95% confidence' information is useful, management should also be informed of the potential losses in case of rare, but still possible, big shocks. With reference to those who have experienced and hopefully survived periods of very high volatility, they have called this measure of risk *stress scenario*.

Earnings-at-risk under 'stress scenarios'

'Those who cannot remember the past are condemned to repeat it.' The management of a bank should be informed about the impact of a rare large change of interest rates on the net interest margin of the bank. For instance, in 2001, Turkey experienced short-term interest rates of 1000% when the liquidity dried up.

$$EAR_{stress} = |gap| \times (\text{big change of rates})$$

It is the task of the risk management team to imagine the very rare but possible large shocks that could impact the interest rates and affect the economy. Some banks have wisely created a 'stress scenarios' committee to select the relevant stress scenarios. An analysis of the economic history of the country or of other countries provides example of large economic shocks. But in the same way as one does not drive a car looking in the rear-view mirror, it is advisable to dream ahead and envision what could be potential shocks.

KEY POINTS

BANKING TRANSACTIONS ARE GROUPED INTO

The banking book (at historical cost)   and   The trading book (marked-to-market)

➡ As far as the P&L is concerned, the banking book creates a net interest margin (NIM), while the trading book generates a change in value.

➡ The repricing gaps help to analyze the impact of interest rate on the net interest margin.

➡ Two measures of risk are reported:
   - at the 95% confidence level; and
   - for stress scenarios.

➡ $EAR = |gap| \times \Delta$ rate

EXERCISE STAGE ELEVEN

Here is the repricing gap table of Bank Alpha.

Repricing date	0–3 months	3–6 months	Non-interest rate sensitive
Assets	100	150	
Deposits	120	100	
Equity			30
Gap	−20	+50	−30
Cumulative gap	−20	+30	0

The volatility of interest rate is at 2% with a confidence level of 95%. That is, the yield curve currently at 8% is unlikely to move (only 5% probability) outside the range 6% – 10%.

In the past ten years, this country has experienced a few rare shocks of 4% moves in the yield curve.

Questions

1 With reference to the net interest margin of the coming quarter (0–3 months), will it improve if the interest rate goes up? Yes or No?

2 With reference to the net interest margin of the second quarter (3–6 months), will it improve if the interest rate goes up? Yes or No?

3 With reference to the net interest margin of the coming quarter (0–3months), calculate the earnings-at-risk for a 95% confidence level.

$$EAR_{95\%} = |gap| \times \Delta R_{5\%} = \ldots\ldots$$

4 With reference to the net interest margin of the second quarter (3–6 months), calculate the earnings-at-risk for a stress scenario.

$$EAR_{stress} = |gap| \times \Delta R_{stress} = \ldots\ldots$$

stage

THE CONTROL OF INTEREST RATE RISK (2): THE SIMULATION MODEL

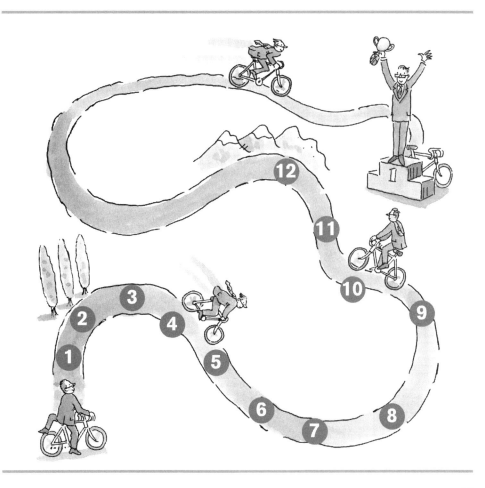

In the previous stage, we analyzed the impact of a change of interest rate on the net interest margin of e-Bank.

In doing so, we made a series of implicit assumptions that are not always valid. We propose to generalize the approach with the introduction of simulation models.

Limits to the use of repricing gaps

In the previous stage, we analyzed the impact of a change of interest rate on the net interest margin of a bank. In this respect, we needed two kinds of information: the *gap* and the *relevant change of interest rate*.

The gap indicates whether there is a net asset position to reprice or whether there is a net debt position to reprice.

Gap = (repriced assets) – (repriced liabilities) *over a specific period of time*

■ A positive gap indicates an excess of short-term assets to reprice.

■ A negative gap indicates an excess of short-term liabilities to reprice.

To measure the risk, the bank must choose a relevant change of interest rate that will cover most of the cases.

$\Delta_{95\%}$ **rate = the relevant change of interest rate that needs to be analyzed**
Risk = EAR$_{95\%}$ = |gap| × ($\Delta_{95\%}$ rate)

There were two implicit assumptions in this analysis:

1. *All interest rates on assets and deposits move by the same magnitude.* We have considered only one change of interest rate, that is assuming that the interest rate on all assets and liabilities would change by the same amount. This is likely to be a fair approximation on the very competitive interbank or corporate markets. But in the retail banking sector, rates can be fairly rigid and inelastic. And even on the interbank market, it can happen that the correlation between two rates is not perfect. The fact that two interest rates with the same maturity do not move exactly in parallel is referred to as *basis risk*.

2. *A static approach.* The analysis is conducted at a very specific moment in time by looking at the current balance sheet. It ignores the impact of interest rates on the volume of deposits and loans over time. For instance, the future volume of consumer loans could be reduced when interest rates increase.

As the assumption of a parallel (identical) movement of interest rates is not always valid, especially in the case of the retail market, the information given by the repricing gaps has to be completed with a *simulation model.*

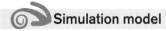

Simulation model

A simulation model works in three steps:

1. *Calculate your repricing table*, that is the repricing dates of all existing assets and liabilities.
2. *Design several economic scenarios*, each of them including:
   - a new interest rate curve (for example over the next two years);
   - a forecast of deposits and loans volumes;
   - the pricing of deposits and loans for that specific curve.
3. *Simulation*. Ask the accountants and computer experts to simulate (forecast) your balance sheet and income statement for each of the scenarios.

The task of the risk manager is to identify the relevant scenarios and to report how the profit of the bank would be affected in each of them.

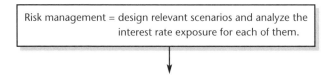

Risk management = design relevant scenarios and analyze the interest rate exposure for each of them.

Thanks to Monte Carlo simulation, millions of interest rate scenarios can be developed, but usually banks look at six or seven different ones that include various yield curves, volume changes and repricing assumptions.

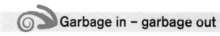

Garbage in – garbage out

It may be useful to underline that if a scenario is irrelevant, the measure of risk made through a simulation model will be irrelevant too. Risk management is not a science, it is an art, the art of designing relevant scenarios.

KEY POINTS

➡ The impact of an interest rate change on the net interest margin of a bank is analyzed through

| The gap | The $\Delta_{95\%}$ rate | A simulation model |

➡ The simulation consists of the forecast of balance sheets and income statements related to different scenarios.

➡ Risk management = design relevant scenarios, analyze the risk, and decide how to limit (cap) the risk.

EXERCISE STAGE TWELVE

Here is the repricing gap table of Alpha Bank.

Repricing date	0–3 months	3–6 months	Non-interest rate sensitive
Assets	100	150	
Deposits	120	100	
Equity			30
Gap	–20	+50	–30
Cumulative gap	–20	+30	0

The volatility of interest rate is at 2% with a confidence level of 95%. In other words, the interbank yield curve, currently at 8%, is unlikely to move (only 5% probability) outside of the range 6–10%.

In the past ten years, if the interest rate on assets has adjusted by 1% for a 1% change in the interbank rate, the cost of deposits has adjusted by only 50 basis points (0.5%), a well-known case of interest inelasticity in the retail market. However, you are concerned that in the future, increased competition from internet banks could raise that elasticity to 0.75.

Questions

1. With reference to the net interest margin of the coming quarter (0–3 months), calculate the earnings-at-risk for a 95% confidence level if the 0.5 elasticity holds.

$EAR_{95\%} = \ldots \ldots$

2. With reference to the net interest margin of the coming quarter (0–3 months), calculate the earnings-at-risk for a 95% confidence level if the 0.75 elasticity holds.

$EAR_{95\%} = \ldots \ldots$

FORWARDS AND FINANCIAL FUTURES

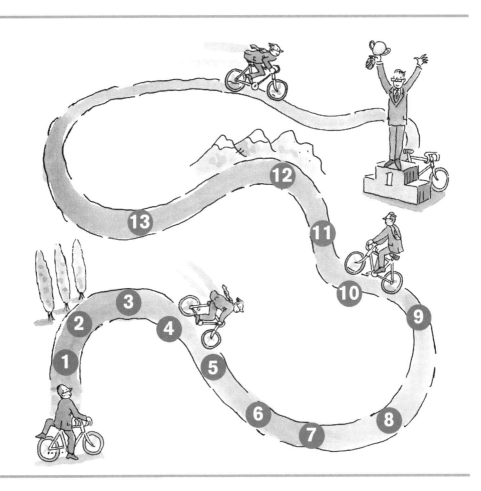

'A good hedge keeps the dog off the yard.'

Now that we know how to measure the interest rate risk exposure, we can introduce some tools to manage the position.

These include forward contracts and financial futures. Options are introduced in Stage 16.

Forward contracts

For many years, banks have been using forward contracts to hedge a risk or to take a position.

A forward is an agreement between two parties to sell a financial instrument (a share, currency, bond) at a future date (the delivery date) at a predetermined price.

EXAMPLE

For instance, let us imagine a contract signed in September between e-Bank and Alpha Bank: e-Bank agrees to buy a 3-month-to-maturity treasury bill next December at a price of 90 fixed today.

Today	December	March
(Price is fixed and	Delivery date	Maturity of
contract signed)	(buy/sell)	underlying bond

It is an off-balance sheet transaction as it is just an agreement between two parties. As discussed in Stage 1, it has no impact on assets and liabilities (the very small transaction costs excepted).

At the delivery date (next December) e-Bank will buy from Alpha bank the bond at the agreed price of 90.

● *If in December the T-bill price went up, e-Bank would have made a profit, the difference between the December market price and the price of the contract (90).*

● *If the price went down, e-Bank would have made a loss.*

In addition to interest rate risk, the forward contract creates a *counterparty risk*. If the counterparty Alpha Bank defaults next December and is unable to sell the treasury bill, e-Bank can still buy the T-bill in the market, but at the price prevailing in December. e-Bank could incur an implicit loss if the December market price is larger than 90, loss which is referred to as the 'replacement' risk, occurring when the asset has to be bought at a price different to the one agreed in the initial September contract.

Financial futures

To reduce the risk of counterparty default, financial futures contracts can be used. They have several characteristics.

1. *A third party involved.* The first characteristic of financial futures is to involve an independent third party in the transaction, the *future exchange*. The contract between e-Bank and Alpha Bank is replaced by two new contracts (legal notion of *novation*) connecting the two banks with the future exchange (Figure 13.1).

Figure 13.1 The role of the future exchange

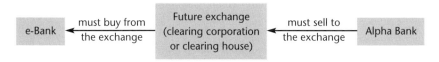

The counterparty risk between the two banks has been replaced by a counterparty risk with the exchange. This one has usually very strong shareholders to guarantee the terms of the transactions.

2. *A better liquidity*. These contracts usually have standard sizes (e.g. contract of $500 000), a standard underlying instrument (for instance a three-month-to-maturity treasury bill), and specific delivery dates (usually four per year, that is March, June, September and December). The market is open every day but delivery dates are few. These standardized contracts force all players to concentrate demand and supply on a few instruments, which improves liquidity. Liquidity is particularly important for specula-tors who want to be able to move in and out of a market very quickly.

Marking-to-market and margin calls

In order to enter a financial future, you have to deposit a margin (a guarantee) with the exchange. At the end of every day, the terms of the contract are adjusted (marked-to-market) to the price prevailing on the future exchange.

For instance, if the price goes up to 91, e-Bank will now have to pay 91 (instead of 90). In compensation, e-Bank will receive a cash payment of 1. In reverse, Alpha Bank will have to use its margin to pay the loss of 1.

Profits and losses are settled on a daily basis (daily margin calls) and the losing party is forced to use its margins to finance the loss, which helps to reduce significantly the risk of default for the exchange and for the market participants. To remain in the market, the losing party will have to transfer cash to meet the margin requirement. This can create a source of liquidity risk that will be discussed in Stage 15.

 Payoffs

Figure 13.2 illustrates the payoffs of a financial future transaction. The dotted line stands for the contract to buy (a so-called *long position*). A profit is made when the price of the underlying instrument goes up. The solid line shows the result of the contract to sell (a *short position*). A profit is made when the price of the underlying instrument goes down.

Figure 13.2 The payoffs of a financial future transaction

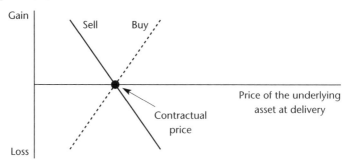

Hedging repricing gaps with futures

In Stage 11, we noticed that the first gap of e-Bank for the coming quarter was –310 (which meant an excess of short-term deposits to reprice). In order to protect e-Bank from an interest rate increase, which would negatively impact the cost of funds, you could use a three-month T-bill future contract with a delivery in the coming quarter.

This hedging strategy aims to generate a profit with the financial future that compensates the loss due to the negative gap. *Should we buy or sell futures?* Since we want to make a profit when the interest rate goes up (the price of bonds goes down), we would sell a future to hedge the position. If the interest rate goes up, we lose money *on-balance sheet* as we need to reprice these excess deposits (the negative gap), but we make a profit *off-balance sheet* with the short financial future position. If the interest rate goes down, the reverse will occur.[1]

---

[1] The authors advise great care in the use of financial futures to hedge a position. There have been several real cases of banks taking futures positions that effectively doubled their risk exposure when they were seeking to hedge the risk.

KEY POINTS

➡ A forward is an agreement between two parties to sell a financial instrument (a share, a currency, a bond) at a future date (the delivery date) at a predetermined price.

Protection against price or interest rate fluctuation

BUT...

Risk of counter-party default

➡ A financial future contract has specific characteristics:

- it involves a third party, the future exchange;
- sizes of contracts are standardized;
- delivery dates are few;
- margin requirements are used to reduce insolvency risk.

➡ The creation of a financial future has helped to increase liquidity while reducing counterparty risk.

Hedging strategy

➡ You can hedge repricing gaps with futures:

- Sell a future if the bank has a negative gap.
- Buy a future if the bank has a positive gap

EXERCISE STAGE THIRTEEN

This exercise builds on the evaluation of interest rate risk (Stage 11) and financial futures (Stage 13).

1. Each cell in the following table represents a particular situation. For instance, the first cell represents a bank with a positive repricing gap at the time when interest rate goes up. Is this a *good* or a *bad* situation for the bank? Enter in the box either GOOD or BAD.

Remember that a repricing gap is the difference between assets being repriced during a specific time period and deposits being repriced.

	Repricing gaps	
	Positive	Negative
Rate up		
Rate down		

2. Each cell in the following table represents a specific financial future position. For instance, in the first cell you have a position to buy a bond at a specific future delivery date at a price fixed today (technically a 'long' position). If the interest rate goes up, is it good or bad for you? Enter in the cell either GOOD or BAD.

	Financial futures	
	Buy (long)	Sell (short)
Rate up		
Rate down		

3. If you want to hedge a risk resulting from a *positive gap*, do you buy or sell financial futures?

If you want to hedge a risk resulting from a *negative gap*, do you want to buy or sell financial futures?

THE CONTROL OF INTEREST RATE RISK (3): THE VALUE OF EQUITY AT RISK

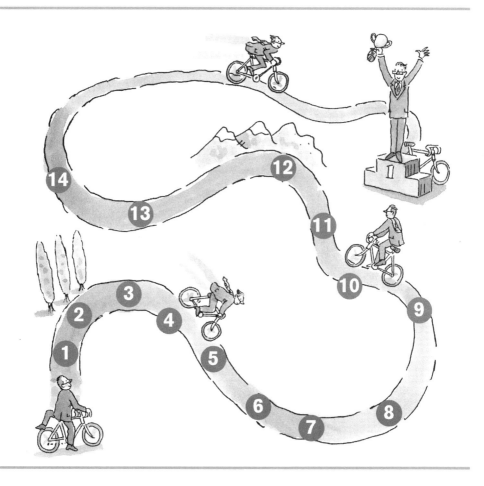

In previous stages, we have analyzed the impact of interest rates on e-Bank's net interest margin.

Here, we provide an alternative and complementary measure of interest rate risk: the value of equity at risk.

 ## Bank solvency and the value of equity

Let us consider a simple balance sheet.

Assets	Deposits
	Equity

The bank is solvent, that is depositors are protected, as long as the value of assets exceeds the value of deposits, or as long as the value of equity is positive:

Value of equity = value of assets – value of deposits

If the interest rate goes up, one would expect a change (Δ) in the value assets, the value of deposits, and the value of equity.

Δ(value of equity) = Δ(value of assets) – Δ(value of deposits)

The risk manager is therefore looking for a measure of the value at risk, that is an easy indicator of the impact of the interest rate on value. *Duration* provides such an indicator.

 **Duration**

For many years, specialists used the maturity of an asset as an indicator of interest rate risk. *For example, the value of a 30-year fixed-rate bond will be more sensitive to interest rates than the value of a one-year-to-maturity bond.* However, they have realized that maturity provides only information on the timing of the very last cash flow to come. It does not take into account the cash flows received earlier (such as interest payments). This is precisely what duration does. It is an *average maturity* that also takes into account the cash flows received in the early life of the asset.

EXAMPLE

10% coupon, three-year-to-maturity bond. Price is equal to 95.2 for an interest rate curve of 12%.

Year 0	Year 1	Year 2	Year 3	Current rate
95.2	10	10	110	12%

Price = 95.2

The duration of that bond is given by the following formula:

$$\text{Duration} = \frac{1 \times \left(\dfrac{10}{1.12}\right) + \left(2 \times \dfrac{10}{1.12^2}\right) + \left(3 \times \dfrac{110}{1.12^3}\right)}{95.2} = 2.728 \text{ years}$$

Duration is the average of years $\left\{\begin{array}{l}\text{One}\\\text{Two}\\\text{Three}\end{array}\right\}$ **weighted by the discounted cash flows.**

Intuitively, duration represents the average maturity of an asset. In this example, the duration of 2.782 years is close to three years because we receive a large cash flow of 110 in Year Three.

Duration has become a very useful measure of the value at risk of an asset since finance specialists have found that the change in price of an asset is the product of three elements: the price, the duration and the change of interest rate.

Δprice = − price × [duration/(1+ R)] × ΔR

Once you know the duration of an asset, you can easily compute the impact of a change of interest rate on the price of that asset. So far we have concerned ourselves with the value at risk of an asset. We now extend the concept to the value of equity at risk.

The value of equity at risk

In order to analyze the impact of interest rates on the change in value of e-Bank's equity, you apply the duration formula to both assets and debt:

Δ(value of equity) = Δ(value of assets) − Δ(value of deposits)

Let us call the assets 'A' and the deposits 'D':

$$\Delta \text{ value of equity} = [- A \times Du_A / (1 + R) \times \Delta R)] - [- D \times Du_D / (1 + R) \times \Delta R)]$$

Playing with mathematics yields this intuitive relation:

$$\Delta \text{ value of equity/equity} = - A/E \times [(Du_A - D/A\ Du_D)/(1 + R)] \times \Delta R$$

Leverage   Difference between the durations (duration gap)   Change of interest rate

$$\Delta \text{ value of equity/equity} = - \text{leverage} \times \text{duration gap} \times \Delta R$$

The percentage change in the value of equity of the bank is the product of three terms: its leverage, the duration mismatch between assets and debt, and the change in interest rate.

Two measures of interest rate risk

Most banks are equipped today with two measures of interest rate risk (Figure 14.1).

Figure 14.1 The two measures of interest rate risk

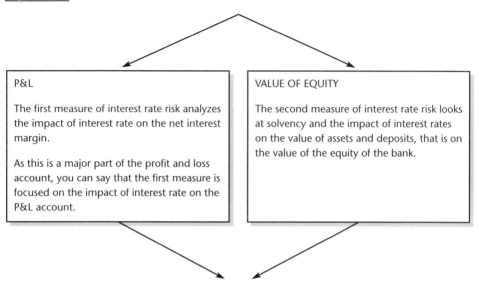

P&L	VALUE OF EQUITY
The first measure of interest rate risk analyzes the impact of interest rate on the net interest margin. As this is a major part of the profit and loss account, you can say that the first measure is focused on the impact of interest rate on the P&L account.	The second measure of interest rate risk looks at solvency and the impact of interest rates on the value of assets and deposits, that is on the value of the equity of the bank.

Although finance specialists would rather focus on the value of equity at risk as it represents the present value of all future cash flows, senior bankers also consider carefully the first measure (impact on the NIM) because of the attention bank analysts pay to short-term profitability and return on equity.

It is advisable to monitor both measures of risk.

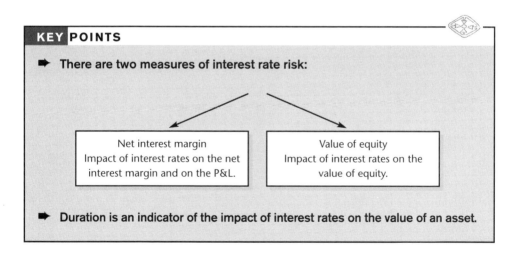

KEY POINTS

➡ **There are two measures of interest rate risk:**

Net interest margin Impact of interest rates on the net interest margin and on the P&L.	Value of equity Impact of interest rates on the value of equity.

➡ **Duration is an indicator of the impact of interest rates on the value of an asset.**

EXERCISE STAGE FOURTEEN

Please note the following information about e-Bank:

- Value of asset:100   (Duration = 5 years)

- Value of debt: 95   (Duration = 1 year)

- Interest rate level: 10%

1. Calculate the current value of the equity of the bank

2. Estimate the percentage change in the value of the bank's equity for an interest rate movement of 2%. You can use the formula discussed in Stage 14.

Δ value of equity/equity $= - A/E \times [Du_A - D/A\ Du_D)/(1 + R)] \times \Delta R$

THE CONTROL OF LIQUIDITY RISK

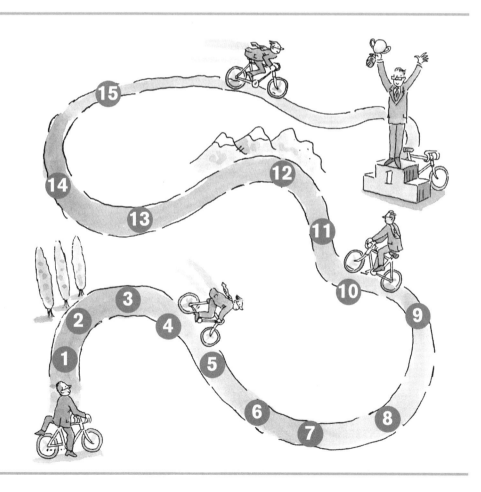

At all times, a bank must be able to meet the cash flow obligations arising from deposit withdrawals and financial commitments.

Banks evaluate liquidity risk in two steps.

The methodology to control liquidity risk is similar to that of the control of interest rate risk. In the latter case, we were concerned with repricing dates and the impact of a change of interest rates on the net interest margin. In this case, we are concerned with the cash position of e-Bank. Two situations will be considered: the 'normal' times and the 'stress scenarios'.

Cash flow gap for 'normal time'

The bank calculates the amount of cash coming in and going out over a fairly short time interval (the coming days) (Table 15.1).

Table 15.1 The net cash flow

−	Interest income
−	interest expense
−/+	margin calls
−	operating expenses
−	tax
+	reimbursement of principal on loans or bonds
−	estimated amount of lending
−	reimbursement of deposits
+	estimated amount of new deposits

If the cash flow is *positive*, there is no liquidity problem.

If the cash flow is *negative*, the bank will have to plan borrowing on the interbank market or proceed with the sale of bonds.

In order to avoid meeting a liquidity problem, the bank will put a cap on the amount of money it needs to borrow over a certain period. For instance, this cap could represent 5% of the deposit base for a one-week cash flow gap.

 Cash flow for 'stress' scenarios

As with the management of interest rate risk, liquidity risk has to be analyzed for the case of a banking crisis. In such a 'stress' case, there will be a 'run' on the bank, with many depositors rushing to cash in their deposits and, possibly, some borrowers being unable to meet their loan repayments.

The net cash outflow arising from such a crisis situation has to be estimated and banks have to make sure that they have enough liquid assets to sell for survival.

Typically, banks want to be able to cope with the crisis for a few days or a week, the time needed for the central bank to inject liquidity into the banking system. To meet these possible 'stress scenarios', banks must meet a liquidity ratio defined as liquid assets over short-term deposits.

Finally, the last measure helping banks to reduce liquidity risk is to ensure a proper diversification of their funding sources so that you would not depend too much on any one of them.

KEY POINTS

➡ Cash flow forecast: banks need to estimate the cash outflow over the coming days, both for 'normal' and 'stress' times.

➡ Liquidity ratio: $\dfrac{\text{Liquid assets}}{\text{Short-term deposits}}$

➡ Diversification of funding sources is needed to reduce the liquidity risk.

EXERCISE STAGE FIFTEEN

Here is e-Bank's current balance sheet. The liquidity risk manager has calculated the liquidity profile of the coming two weeks.

Balance sheet

Loans	300,000	Customers' deposits	400,000
Bonds	250,000	Interbank	100,000
		Equity	50,000
Total	550,000	Total	550,000

Liquidity profile

	One week	Two weeks
Interest income	1000	1000
− Interest expense	− 700	− 700
− Operating expenses	− 100	− 100
− Tax	− 0	− 0
+ Reimbursement of principal on loans and bonds	+ 30,000	+ 30,000
− Estimated amount of lending	− 25,000	− 35,000
− Reimbursement of deposits	− 40,000	− 10,000
+ Estimated amount of new deposits	+ 10,000	+ 10,000
Net cash flows	− 24,800	− 4800
Cumulative net cash flows	− 24,800	− 29,600

1. e-Bank's liquidity risk policy is as follows:
   - the one-week liquidity gap cannot exceed 5% of the customers' deposit base;
   - the two-week cumulative liquidity gap cannot exceed 10% of the customers' deposits.

   Does e-Bank meet the one-week liquidity rule: Yes or No?
   Does e-Bank meet the two-week liquidity rule: Yes or No?

2. How can e-Bank improve its liquidity position? Suggest a portfolio transaction that will enhance the liquidity.

3. If there were a run on the bank, it is estimated that there would be an additional net cash outflow of 220,000 in the coming seven days. Does e-Bank meet the liquidity stress policy which wants the bank to be able to survive for one week in case of a run on its deposits?

stage

16

OPTIONS

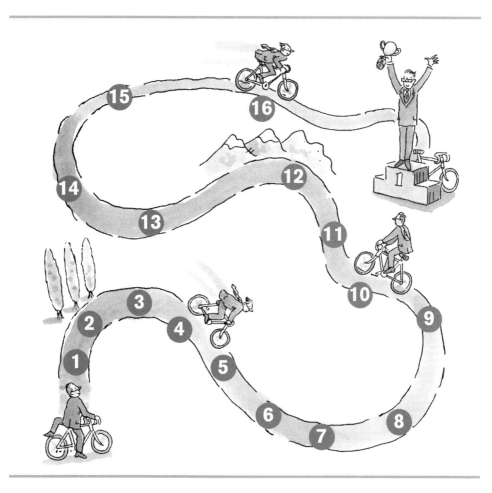

We have already met two instruments to hedge interest rate exposure: forwards and financial futures.
Here we introduce a third one: options.

To introduce options, it is first convenient to refer to forward and futures contracts.

 Forwards and futures

As we discussed in Stage 13, forwards and financial futures are agreements to buy (or sell) a government bond at a price fixed today (say 90) with a delivery date in the future (Figure 16.1).

Figure 16.1 Forwards and financial futures

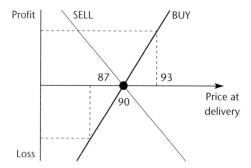

- If the bond price at delivery date exceeds 90, there is a gain when you buy a future.

- If the bond price falls to 87, there would be a loss since we would have to pay 90 for an asset which is worth only 87.

OPTIONS

As the future graph indicates clearly, the downside risk of buying a future is large if you take a wrong position. A major advantage of an option is to keep the profit potential while limiting your downside risk.

A call option is a right to buy a financial asset at a price fixed today (the exercise price or strike) with delivery at a future date.

A put option is a right to sell a bond at a price fixed today with a delivery in the future.

The difference between an option and a financial future stands in one word. The option is a *right*, while the future is an *agreement*. As the holder of an option may or may not exercise his right, an option will be exercised only if it brings a gain to the holder of this option.

Call option

A call option is a right to *buy* a financial asset at a price fixed today (the exercise price or strike) with delivery at a future date (Figure 16.2).

Figure 16.2 A call option

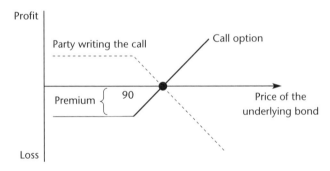

On the right side of the exercise price of 90, the bond price goes up and the call option is exercised. On the left side of the figure, the bond price falls below 90 and the option is not exercised. In that case, the only loss will be the premium paid to buy the option.

An option is therefore a convenient tool to make a profit while keeping a limited downside risk.

Note that for the party selling (writing) the call, the payoff (dashed line) is completely different. The writer of the call keeps the premium if the option is not being exercised. If it is exercised, it could end up with very heavy losses. One can compare the business of writing options with the business of underwriting insurance. In that business you collect upfront an insurance premium and keep it if there is no casualty. However, if there is one, the insurance liability could be large.

Put option

A put option is a right to *sell* a bond at a price fixed today with a delivery in the future (Figure 16.3).

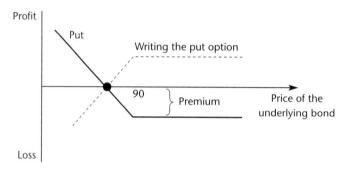

Figure 16.3 **A put option**

On the left side of the exercise price of 90, the bond price goes down and the put option is exercised. On the right side of the graph, the bond price increases over 90 and the option is not exercised. In that case, the only loss will be the premium paid to buy the option.

Note that for the party selling (writing) the put, the payoff scheme (dashed line) is completely different. The writer of the put keeps the premium if the option is not exercised. If it is exercised, it could end up with heavy losses.

 ## Volatility, a new source of risk

The value (premium paid) of an option today depends on how likely it is that the price of the bond will be different from the exercise price, and by how much. Complex formulae have been devised but, intuitively, one can guess that the option premium will include the current price of the bond, the exercise price, and its volatility (the standard deviation of the probability distribution of the value of the underlying bond). Indeed, when the volatility is large, there is a greater chance of a large price movement and of a large profit.

Banks holding or writing options are facing a new type of risk: the value of their option portfolio may change when:

- the price of bonds changes;
- the volatility of bond prices changes.

To manage option risk, specialists of option portfolios simulate the changes in option value for both a change in the price of the underlying bond and a change in the volatility.

KEY POINTS

➡ An option is a right to buy (call) or sell (put) a specific amount of a financial asset, with delivery at a specific date in the future, at a given price fixed today.

➡ As it is a right and not an obligation, the holder of the option keeps the profit potential while limiting the downside risk. However, the writer (seller) of the option faces a significant downside risk.

➡ Changes in bonds prices and volatility can both impact the value of an option.

EXERCISE STAGE SIXTEEN

A call option to buy a bond at a price of 85 at the end of next year is trading at a premium of 6. You buy this call option.

1. If interest rates go down and the bond price ends up at 95 at the end of next year, what is your net revenue?

2. If interest rates go up and the bond price ends up at 80 at the end of next year, what is your net revenue?

3. If you believe that interest rates will go up, which investment strategy do you recommend for call options?

ASSET AND LIABILITY
MANAGEMENT: AN ART,
NOT A SCIENCE

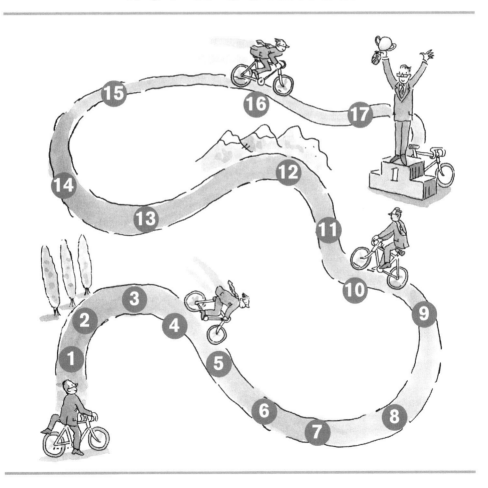

We have completed our review of the various ALM tools needed to control profitability and risks in a commercial bank.

A summary of the most important ALM tools will highlight that ALM is more an art than a science.

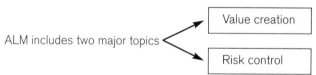

ALM includes two major topics

- Value creation
- Risk control

The control of profit and value creation

There are just a few key concepts or building blocks to keep in mind. At the overall bank level, senior management needs to ensure that:

Market value of shares > equity invested by shareholders.

Technically, this demands that the long-term return on equity exceeds the cost of equity:

Return on equity > cost of equity

Where the cost of equity represents the expected return that shareholders could obtain from alternative investment opportunities.

At profit centre level, a measure of performance consistent with the overall objectives of the bank needs to be developed.

Economic profit = economic value added (EVA)
= allocated profit – cost of allocated equity

Three key issues concern the choice of a transfer price for deposits and loans, the allocation of equity to profit centres, and the creation of provisions for credit risk. The transfer price must send the right signal to managers; in many countries, it is estimated with the matched-maturity market rate. The allocation of equity could be based on regulation or, preferably, on an analysis of the risks taken by e-Bank. Intuitively, equity in any corporation is needed to absorb potential losses so as to remain solvent. Provisions are needed to capture the potential future losses and to give the right incentives to lenders.

The risk-adjusted measure of performance has major implications for loan pricing.

Pricing loans

- The pricing of loans has to ensure value creation.
- We have shown that the interest on loans should incorporate a reward for shareholders (the 'equity' spread) and a spread for expected credit risk.
- The size of the credit spread will be driven by the probability of default and by the expected recovery rate in case of default.

Loan securitization

We discussed that it is sometimes less costly to sell a loan (securitization) than to keep it on the balance sheet. Not only does this help to save capital, it can also improve liquidity and the diversification of credit risks.

The control of interest rate risk

We have shown that there are two ways to look at interest rate risk.

- The first one is very much driven by the impact of interest rate on the profit and loss account.
- An alternative is to focus on the value of equity of the entire bank.

Since the last approach captures both short-term and long-term risks, it is recommended to use both approaches.

Volatility of interest rate is a key variable. Two sets of scenarios should be foreseen:

- volatility under 'normal' time;
- volatility at a time of crisis (stress scenario).

The control of liquidity risk

At all times, the bank must ensure that it can meet its commitments (such as salaries or tax payment, deposits repayment or loan commitments) both in 'normal' times and in rare cases of stress scenarios.

Congratulations! You have just completed the final stage of *Asset & Liability Management, A Guide to Value Creation and Risk Control*.

Two final thoughts:

ALM is not a science. Although it relies on mathematics and statistics, you should always be aware of the assumptions underlying these models. For instance, what scenarios have been analyzed for the 'stress' case? What assumptions does one make about liquidity and the ease of closing a trading position? All of these assumptions should be verified and accepted by senior management. Remember the saying: 'Garbage in, garbage out'.

ALM is fundamental to a proper allocation of capital and human resources to those activities that create value. ALM is fundamental to control risks. In very much the same way as you would not send a rocket to the moon without proper control instruments, you do not manage a bank and the deposits of millions of investors without a proper ALM system.

Appendix

SOFTWARE

1. How to get started

You will find enclosed a CD-ROM. To run the program, just install the CD-ROM in the driver. The program will start by itself.

If this CD-ROM does not launch automatically when you insert the disk, double-click 'My Computer' followed by your CD-ROM drive's icon, and then double-click the file 'ALM.EXE'. Alternatively, select 'START', 'RUN' and enter 'r:ALM' where 'r' is the letter of your CD-ROM drive.

2. Specifications

To use the program, you will need an IBM-compatible computer with Microsoft Windows 95, 98, Me, NT, 2000 Professional (or latest version).

You are advised to work on a 'full screen' mode.

3. Online help

At the start of the ALM program, you will read the introduction and a screen which explains the navigation tools. You will be able to access this page again whenever you need it by clicking on the icon.

The 'Help' file explains the functions of all the various buttons and icons available in the program, as well as how to navigate.

4. Navigation

The program will show you how to navigate as the different navigation icons are presented in the introduction. It is extremely flexible and user friendly. Indeed, just after the introduction you will find a road map presenting the 17 stages of the program. You can choose the stage you want to work on just by clicking on it (our advice is to take them in logical order). The program is divided into two main and distinct parts: value creation with Stages One to Ten, and risk management with Stages Eleven to Seventeen).

Each stage is subdivided into four sections:

- the introductory page announces that stage's topic;
- the concepts give explanations of the new ALM tools;
- the key points give a summary of the stage's main lessons;
- the exercise allows you to apply the concepts.

When entering answers to an exercise, you can click on the 'magnifying glass' button to check your answers. Green indicates that it is correct; red indicates an error.

If you click on the 'bulb lamp', the computer will show you how to calculate the correct answer thanks to an animated explanation.

You can advance from page to page in the program by using the 'next' button or the 'return' key. At the end of every stage (i.e. at the end of the exercises), you will be invited to go back to the road map. To do so, just click on the road map icon.

 **5. Printing**

You can print any page of the program by activating that page and then clicking on the print icon.

Warning: all possible efforts have been made to test this CD ROM and the software. However, in no case can the authors be held responsible for damages of any type resulting from the direct or indirect use of this application.

Appendix

ANSWERS TO EXERCISES

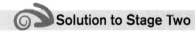
Solution to Stage Two

Consider a bank with an initial equity of 100, an ROE of 10%, and a life of three years. The profit is paid every year as a dividend plus a closing dividend of 110 at the end of three years. Compute the market value and value creation for the cases when the market discounts at 12%, 10%, and 8%.

	Year 1	Year 2	Year 3
Cash flow accruing to investors	10	10	110

a) Market value at 12%
$$= \frac{10}{(1+0.12)} + \frac{10}{(1+0.12)^2} + \frac{110}{(1+0.12)^3} = 95.2$$

Value creation (destruction) $= 95.2 - 100 = -4.8$

b) Market value at 10%
$$= \frac{10}{(1+0.1)} + \frac{10}{(1+0.1)^2} + \frac{110}{(1+0.1)^3} = 100$$

Value creation $= 100 - 100 = 0$

c) Market value at 8%
$$= \frac{10}{(1+0.08)} + \frac{10}{(1+0.08)^2} + \frac{110}{(1+0.08)^3} = 105.15$$

Value creation $= 105.15 - 100 = 5.15$

Managerial lesson: to create value, the ROE must exceed the market discount rate, the cost of equity.

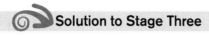Solution to Stage Three

The balance sheet and income statement of your bank are as follows:

Balance sheet (end of the year, $ million)

Assets	110	Debt (including deposits)	105
		Equity	5
Total	110	Total	110

Income statement ($ million)

Interest income	8.2
Fees	0.8
– Interest expenses	–5.25
– Provisions for bad debts	–1.3
– Operating expenses	–1.1
Profit before tax	1.35
– Taxes	–0.54
Profit after tax	0.81

Solutions to ratios are the following:

Return on equity
$$= \frac{0.81}{5} = 16.2\%$$

Earnings on assets
$$= \frac{(8.2 + 0.8 - 1.3)}{110} = 7\%$$

Cost of debt
$$= \frac{5.25}{105} = 5\%$$

Operating expenses ratio
$$= \frac{1.1}{110} = 1\%$$

Leverage (D/E)
$$= \frac{105}{5} = 21$$

Tax rate
$$= \frac{0.54}{1.35} = 40\%$$

We can verify that:

ROE = profit after tax/equity = 0.81/5 = 16.2%

$$
\begin{aligned}
\text{ROE} \ &= (\text{EOA} - \text{OE}) \times (1{-}t) + (\text{EOA} - \text{COD} - \text{OE}) \times (\text{D/E}) \times (1{-}t) \\
&= (7\% - 1\%) \times (1{-}0.4) + (7\% - 5\% - 1\%) \times (21) \times (1{-}0.4) \\
&= 3.6\% + 12.6\% \\
&= 16.2\%
\end{aligned}
$$

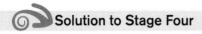

Solution to Stage Four

The allocated profit after tax of the corporate banking division is $4 million. An equity of 20 million has been allocated to this profit centre.

Compute the RAROC, the cost of equity and the EVA knowing that the risk-free rate on government bonds is 10% and that the market demands a risk premium of 5% on bank shares.

Solutions are:

$$RAROC \quad = \frac{4}{20} = 20\%$$

Cost of equity = 10% + 5% = 15%

EVA = 4 − (15% × 20) = 1

Golden rule for value creation:

Value is created by the corporate banking unit whenever the RAROC of 20% exceeds the cost of equity of 15%, or when the EVA of 1 million is positive.

Solution to Stage Five

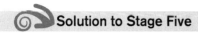 Effective return net of reserve requirement
= interbank rate × (1 – reserve requirement)

For instance, for the one-year interbank rate of 3% and a reserve requirement of 10%, the effective rate is 2.7% (3% × (1 – 10%)).

Net interest margin on deposits
Net interest margin on deposits of 100 = (2.7% – 1.7%) × 100   = 1
Net interest margin on deposits of 200 = (3.15% – 2.15%) × 200 = 2
Total net interest margin on deposits =   1 + 2 = 3

Net interest margin on loans
Net interest margin on loans of 200 = (6% – 4%) × 200 = 4
Net interest margin on loans of 300 = (8% – 5%) × 300 = 9
Total net interest margin on loans = 4 + 9 = 13
Total net interest margin = margin on deposits + margin on loans
$$= 3 + 13 = 16$$

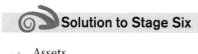

Solution to Stage Six

Assets		Liabilities and shareholders' equity	
Reserves with central bank	60	Demand deposits	750
Mortgage loans	525	Term deposits	450
Corporate loans	450	Interbank deposits	370
Interbank loans	375	Subordinated debt	25
Government bonds	195	Equity	55
Fixed assets	45		
Total	1650	Total	1650

The risk-weighed assets are calculated as follows:

$$\text{RWA} = 0\% \times (60 + 195) + 20\% \times (375) + 50\% \times (525) + 100\% \times (450 + 45) = 832.5$$

Tier 1 capital: $55 / 832.5 = 6.61\%$
Tier 2 capital: $25 / 832.5 = 3.0\%$

BIS capital ratio = Tier 1 + Tier 2 = $6.61\% + 3.0\% = 9.61\%$

Solution to Stage Seven

Equity = present value of loan transaction

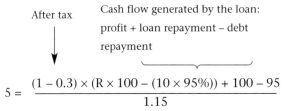

After tax

Cash flow generated by the loan:
profit + loan repayment – debt
repayment

$$5 = \frac{(1 - 0.3) \times (R \times 100 - (10 \times 95\%)) + 100 - 95}{1.15}$$

Break-even loan rate = R = 10.57%

'Equity' spread = loan rate – interbank rate = 10.57% – 10% = 0.57%

Solution to Stage Eight

Part one solution

With R= 14%, the present value of expected cash flows is equal to the present value of cash flows in Year One (certain cash flows as there is no risk of default in Year One) and the present value of expected cash flows in Year Two (uncertain cash flows as there is a risk of default in Year Two).

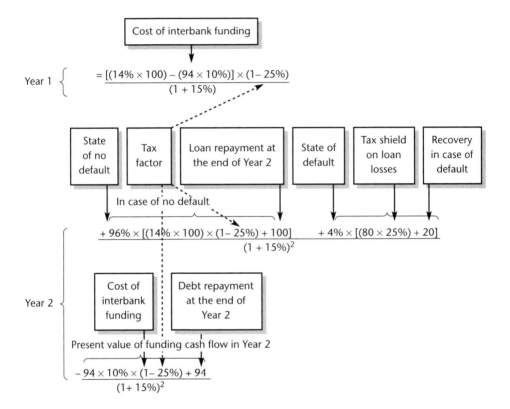

The present value of expected cash flows = 8.01 > 6 (equity invested). Value is being created with a loan priced at 14%.

Part two solution

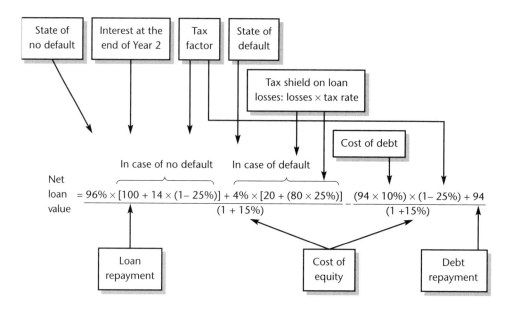

Net loan value = 5.77

At the beginning of the year, the equity invested was 6. As it is now valued at 5.77, there has been a reduction in value of 0.23 during the year, and the profit of the loan should be measured as follows:

Profit on the loan = interest margin after tax + change in net value

$$= (1 - 0.25) \times \{(14\% \times 100) - (10\% \times 94)\} + (5.77 - 6) = 3.45 - 0.23 = 3.22^{(1)}$$

---

[1] An alternative is to create a gain in Year Zero since the net value of the loan was 8.01 when the equity invested was 6 (gain = 8.01 − 6 = 2.01). In that case, the loss of value in Year One would be (5.77 − 8.01 = 2.24).

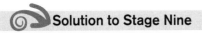 **Solution to Stage Nine**

Investors will evaluate the loan taking into account the expected return available on corporate bonds with similar risk, that is 8%:

$$\text{Value} = \frac{10}{1.08} + \frac{110}{(1.08)^2} = 103.57$$

Capital gain = 103.57 − 100 = 3.57

Solution to Stage Eleven

1. The answer is No. There is a negative gap of –20, indicating a net excess of deposits to reprice. If the interest rate increases, the net interest margin of the first quarter will decrease because the cost of funds will then be larger.

2. The answer is Yes. There is a positive cumulative gap of +30, indicating a net excess of assets to reprice. That is, if the interest rate goes up and remains higher, the interest margin of the second quarter will be affected by the repricing of the deposits of the first quarter (–20), but the repricing of +50 of net assets in the second quarter creates an overall (cumulative) gap of +30 relevant for the interest margin. If the interest rate goes up, the net interest margin of the second quarter will increase because revenues will increase.

3. $EAR_{95\%}$ in the first quarter = $|gap| \times (\Delta_{95\%} \text{ rate})/4 = (20 \times 2\%)/4 = 0.1$
   We divide by 4 to put the EAR on a quarterly basis.

4. EAR_{stress} in the second quarter = gap × (big change of rates)/4
   $$= (30 \times 4\%)/4 = 0.3$$

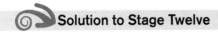

Solution to Stage Twelve

1. $EAR_{95\%}$ = [repricing asset × ($\Delta_{95\%}$ asset rate)] –
[repricing deposits × ($\Delta_{95\%}$ deposit rate)]

= $|(100 \times 2\%) - (120 \times 0.5 \times 2\%)|/4 = |2 - 1.2|/4 = 0.2$

2. $EAR_{95\%}$ = |[repricing asset × ($\Delta_{95\%}$ asset rate)] –

[repricing deposits × ($\Delta_{95\%}$ deposit rate)]|

= $|(100 \times 2\%) - (120 \times 0.75 \times 2\%)|/4 = |2 - 1.8|/4 = 0.05$

If you compare these results to the answers given in Stage Eleven, you will realize that the elasticity of interest rates to a change in interbank rate can have a significant impact on the evaluation of the interest rate exposure. ALM is an art as it relies not only on mathematics but also on relevant assumptions.

Solution to Stage Thirteen

 1.

	Repricing gaps	
	Positive	Negative
Rate up	Good	Bad
Rate down	Bad	Good

In the case of a positive gap in which the assets coming for repricing are larger than the debt being repriced, an increase in the interest rate level will be *good* for you as the additional interest income will exceed the additional interest expense. In reverse, a drop in the interest rate level will be *bad* for you.

In the case of a negative gap in which the deposits coming for repricing are larger than the asset being repriced, an increase in the interest rate level will be *bad* for you as the additional interest expense will exceed the additional interest income. In reverse, a drop in interest rate level will be *good* for you.

2.

	Financial futures	
	Buy (long)	Sell (short)
Rate up	Bad	Good
Rate down	Good	Bad

When interest rates go up, the price of bonds goes down. In that case, you prefer to sell a future at the high price rather than being forced to buy at the high price.

When interest rates go down, the price of bonds goes up. In that case, you prefer to buy a future at the low price rather than being forced to sell at the low price.

3. If you want to hedge a risk resulting from a positive gap, you *buy* financial futures. In that case, you will square your position. If interest rates go down, the loss of revenue on balance sheet will be offset by a gain on the future. And vice versa if interest rates increase.

If you want to hedge a risk resulting from a negative gap, you *sell* financial futures. In that case, you will square your position. If interest rates go up, the loss of revenue on balance sheet will be offset by a gain on the future. And vice versa if interest rates decrease.

Solution to Stage Fourteen

1. Economic value = value of assets – value of debt = 100 – 95 = 5

2. Change in value of equity:

Δ **value of equity/equity** $= - A/E \times [(Du_A - D/A\ Du_D)/(1 + R)] \times \Delta R$

Δ **value of equity/5** $= - 100/5 \times [5 - (95/100) \times 1/(1.1)] \times 0.02 = - 7.36/5$
$\qquad\qquad\qquad = - 147.2\%$

In this exercise, an increase in the interest rate of 2% would completely destroy the bank's equity, meaning that the value of assets would no longer cover the value of deposits.

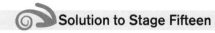Solution to Stage Fifteen

1. e-Bank does not meet the one-week liquidity policy as the estimated cash outflows over the first week (24 800) exceeds 5% of the deposit base

   (400,000 × 5% = 20,000).

   e-Bank meets the two-week liquidity policy as the cumulative cash outflows (29,600) are less than 10% of the customers' deposit base

   (400,000 × 10% = 40,000)).

2. One way to improve the liquidity of the first week is to borrow one-year maturity for 10,000 and buy a one-week bond. At reimbursement of the bond, an additional liquidity of 10,000 would be available, reducing the one-week liquidity gap to 14,800 (24,800 – 10,000).

3. In case of a bank run, the one-week liquidity gap under this stress scenario would be 244,800. This could be funded by the sale of the liquid bond portfolio of 250,000.

Solution to Stage Sixteen

1. If the bond price goes up to 95, I exercise the option (that is to buy the bond at 85), sell it on the market for a profit of 10 (95–85). Given the premium expense of 6, my net revenue is 4.

2. If the bond price goes down to 80, I shall not use the option since it is cheaper to buy the bond directly at its market price. I would have lost then the option premium of 6.

3. If I believe that interest rates will increase (i.e. the bond price is falling), I would sell (write) call options for a premium. If these options are not exercised, my profit would be the option premium received.

Appendix

GLOSSARY

AFGAP: Association Française de Gestion Actif Passif (French association of ALM specialists).

ALCO: the Asset & Liability Committee, in charge of asset and liability management, includes the senior management of a bank: CEO, heads of business units (such as retail and corporate), head of treasury, head of accounting and control, and the chief economist. In some banks, the ALCO is called GALCO (Group Asset & Liability Committee), ALMAC (Asset & Liability Management & Action Committee) or ALPCO (Asset & Liability Policy Committee).

ALM: asset and liability management incorporates the set of techniques to control value creation and risks in a bank.

ALMA: Asset Liability Management Association. British association of ALM specialists.

American option: an option that may be exercised at any time up to and including the expiration date.

Asset & Liability Committee: *see* ALCO.

Asset and liability management: *see* ALM.

Bank for International Settlements: located in Basle (Switzerland), the BIS acts as the bank of central banks. It is host of the secretariat of the Basle Committee on Banking Supervision.

Bank run: refers to a situation of banking crisis in which depositors rush ('run') to the bank to withdraw their deposits. This creates a severe liquidity problem.

Banking book: bank activities are classified into two groups – the banking book and the trading book. The banking book includes the loans, some bonds, and deposits. Its key accounting characteristic is that assets are recorded at historical cost.

Basis point: one-hundredth of 1% (0.0001).

Basis risk: refers to the fact that two interest rates with identical maturity do not move by the same amount. A classical case is the retail markets in which deposit rates or credit card rates are notoriously inelastic. Another case is the lack of correlation between government treasury bills and the rate on interbank deposits.

Basle Committee on Banking Supervision: committee of banking supervisory authorities which was established by central bank governors of the group of ten countries in 1975. It consists of senior representatives of bank supervisory authorities and central banks from Belgium, Canada, France, Germany, Italy, Japan, Luxembourg, Netherlands, Sweden, Switzerland, the United Kingdom and the United States.

Basle 2: refers to a proposal by the Basle Committee for new capital rules that might apply in 2005.

BIS: *see* Bank for International Settlements.

Book value of equity: value of equity reported in the balance sheet. It includes the paid-in capital and the accumulated retained earnings.

Call option: a right to buy an asset at a specific date in the future at a prede-termined price (the exercise price).

Capital ratio: refers to the ratio of bank capital over some measure of assets.

Cash flow: represents an amount of money flowing in or out of a company over a certain period of time.

CDs: certificates of deposit. These are short-term bonds issued by banks.

Clearing house: an organization which registers, monitors, matches and guarantees dealings between members and carries out financial settlements.

COD: cost of debt is one of the drivers of the return on equity (ROE). It is defined as total interest expenses divided by the total debt of the bank.

COE: cost of equity. This is the minimum return demanded by shareholders on their equity investment. It represents the return that shareholders could earn on alternative investment opportunities. It is often estimated as the sum of the current interest rate on risk-free government bonds plus a risk premium to recognize the riskiness of shares.

Collateral: a security or cash provided to secure the performance of an obligation.

Commodities: this refers to real goods traded by banks, such as gold, silver or oil.

Confidence interval: for instance a 95% (or 99%) confidence interval states that there is only 5% (1%) probability that a variable could exceed a particu-lar threshold.

Contingent claim: any contractual arrangement entered into at a point in time for the sale or purchase of some asset or good at some date in the future contingent on a specific event taking place.

Convexity: property associated with fixed-income security that as the inter-est rate decreases, the price of the security increases at an increasing rate.

Cooke capital ratio: regulatory capital ratio established by the Basle Committee in 1988. Named after Peter Cooke, head of banking supervision at the Bank of England and chairman of the Basle Committee at the time.

Core capital: *see* Tier 1.

Correlation: a statistical measure of the degree of relationship between two variables. This standardized measure is bounded by 1 and –1. A correlation of +1 indicates that two variables go up and down together. A correlation of –1 indicates that they move in opposite directions. A correlation close to zero indicates no clear relationship.

Cost-income ratio: operating expenses divided by gross revenue.

Counterparty: buyer or seller under a contingent claim. Commonly associated with forwards, futures, options or swaps.

Counterparty risk: the risk that the other party to a contractual arrangement will not fulfil the terms of the contract.

Credit equivalent risk: amount representing the credit risk exposure in off-balance sheet transactions. In the case of derivatives, it represents the potential cost at current market prices of replacing the contract in the case of default by the counterparty.

Credit risk: represents the losses that could be incurred on a loan due to partial reimbursement of the promised balance.

Defeasance period: in the context of trading, this refers to the numbers of days needed to close a position. It can be very short (one day) in liquid markets, but can be longer in illiquid markets (also called 'holding period').

Delivery date: date at which the asset or commodity has to be delivered to fulfil the terms of the contract.

Derivatives: refers to contract between two parties for which the payoffs are derived from the price of an asset of from an interest rate. It includes swaps, forwards, financial futures or options.

Discount rate: this is the interest rate to be used in discounting. It represents the opportunity investment rate that is available to an investor. It includes the interest rate on risk-free bonds plus a risk premium.

Discounting: the discounted value of a cash flow represents the value today of a cash flow received n-years from now. It can be interpreted as the amount of cash needed today for an investment that will deliver the cash flow n-years from now.

Duration: the duration of a bond is its average life. It is defined as the sum of each year in which a cash flow is received, weighted by the relative importance of the discounted cash flow in that year.

EAR: *see* earnings-at-risk.

Earnings-at-risk (EAR): this represents the impact of an unexpected change of interest rate on the profit of a bank. It is also called income-at-stake (IAS) or dollar-at-risk (DAR).

Economic capital: it represents the amount of equity that should be allocated to a profit centre. The logic is that equity is necessary in any business firm to act as a buffer to prevent bankruptcy. Equity is thus necessary to cover the unexpected losses. One refers also to risk-based capital.

Economic profit: the profit allocated to a profit centre reduced by the cost of equity allocated to that centre (also called economic value added).

Economic value added (EVA): the profit allocated to a profit centre reduced by the cost of equity allocated to that centre (also called economic profit).

Economic value of bank: represents the discounted value of after-tax future cash flows. It represents the fair value of the equity of a bank, and is equal to the current value of all assets minus the current value of debt plus the value of all off-balance sheet claims.

Efficiency ratio: *see* cost-income ratio.

EOA: earnings on assets is one of the drivers of the ROE. It is defined as total earnings (interest income plus fees minus credit risk provisions) divided by total assets.

EP: *see* economic profit.

Equity: the amount of money invested by shareholders in a company. It includes the paid-in capital at the time of issue plus the retained earnings accumulated over time.

European option: an option that may be exercised only at the expiration date of the contract.

EVA: *see* economic value added.

Exchange: a place where supply meets demands. For instance, a stock exchange to trade shares or a future exchange to trade futures contracts. Some examples include the CME (Chicago Mercantile Exchange), LIFFE (London International Financial Futures Exchange), MATIF (Marché à Terme International de France) and SIMEX in Singapore.

Exercise date: as relates to options, the price at which an option is exercisable.

Exercise price: as relates to options, the price at which an option is exercised.

Expiration date: the maturity date of an option contract.

Fair value: this represents the likely price at which an asset (or debt) could be sold on financial markets. It is estimated either from market prices when these are available or with the discounted value of future cash flows. The accountants are careful to refer to *fair* value (not to *market* value) to indicate that these are only estimates of prices.

Forward: a contract traded over-the counter that gives the holder the obligation to buy or sell a specified amount of commodities or securities at a predetermined price and date in the future.

Forward rate: a rate that will be applicable at a future date.

Future: a contract traded on an exchange that gives the holder the obligation to buy or sell a specific amount of commodities or securities at a stated price and date in the future.

Gap: *see* liquidity gap or repricing gap.

General provisions: *see* provisions for credit risk.

Gross revenue: interest income plus fees minus interest expenses.

Guarantee: an undertaking by a bank (the guarantor) to stand behind the current obligation of a third party and to carry out these obligations should the third party fail to do so.

Haircut: refers to the part of a security's value which, for conservative reasons, may not be used to meet a collateral requirement.

Holding period: in the context of trading, this refers to the number of days needed to close a position. It can be very short (one day) in liquid markets, but can be longer in illiquid markets (also called 'defeasance period').

Institutional investor: refers to large investors such as pensions funds, life insurance companies, mutual funds or other banks.

Interbank rate: interest rate at which banks lend to one another. One refers to LIBOR (London interbank offered rate) as the rate at which international banks in London are willing to lend to another bank. One refers to LIBID as the rate at which international banks in London are borrowing from another bank. Interbank rates in other countries are referred to as EURIBOR (for the eurozone), KLIBOR (Kuala Lumpur), BIBOR (Bahrein), SIBOR (Saudi Arabia), HIBOR (Hong Kong) …

Interest margin: difference between interest income received on loans and bonds and interest expenses paid in deposits and debt.

Interest rate curve: *see* yield curve.

Interest rate risk: refers to the impact of an unexpected movement of the interest rate on the profit of a bank or on the economic value of equity.

Inverted yield curve: refers to the particular shape of a yield curve with short-term interest rates higher than long-term rates.

Investment portfolio: refers to the portfolio of bonds that a bank intends to keep for a long period. In several countries, it can be booked at historical acquisition cost.

Leverage: this is one of the main drivers of the return on equity (ROE). It is defined as total debt divided by equity (called 'gearing' in some countries).

LIBID: *see* interbank rate.

LIBOR: *see* interbank rate.

Liquidity gap: the net cash outflow or inflow over a certain period such as one day or one week; it allows the calculation of the borrowing requirement over a certain period.

Liquidity risk: refers to the risk of not having affordable cash to meet imperative obligations such as the reimbursement of a deposit or the payment of taxes.

Loss given default (LGD): this is the part of the promised payment that is not being paid when a borrower defaults.

Margin: security deposit necessary to maintain a position in a derivative contract. Margins are usually met with a deposit of cash or with marketable securities.

Margin call: notification to an account holder that the margin account has fallen below the necessary level, so that the margin must be re-established to its proper level.

Mark-to-market: the operation of calculating the fair value of a trading book from quoted market prices or from discounted cash flows.

Market-to-book value ratio: the market value of shares divided by the book value of equity. If the ratio is above one, it is indicative of value creation as the market value of shares is larger than the equity invested by shareholders.

Market value of shares: this is the value of each share multiplied by the number of shares outstanding.

Maturity: the date of the last payment on an asset or debt.

Monte Carlo simulation: a computer-based method that generates automatically a very large number (in the order of thousands) of economic scenarios. This allows the impact of economic scenarios on the future income statements and balance sheets of a bank to be analyzed.

Net interest margin: interest income earned on loans or bonds minus interest expenses paid on deposits and other types of debt.

Netting: the replacement of a series of contracts between two (or several) parties by a new contract. Legal technique used to reduce counterparty risk.

NIM: *see* net interest margin.

Note issuance facilities (NIFs): an arrangement whereby a borrower may draw funds up to a prescribed limit over an extended period by repeated issues to the market of, for example, three or six-month promissory notes.

Notional: in the context of derivatives, this refers to the principal on a contract.

Novation: satisfaction and discharging of existing contractual obligations by the substitution of new contractual obligations. For instance, in a future contract, the obligations between two parties is replaced by two obligations with a third party, the exchange (from the latin word *nova*).

Off-balance sheet: includes all banking transactions that do not appear on the balance sheet of a bank as an asset or as a debt. It includes all the commitments for which a cash flow arises conditional on a specific event. For instance, a loan guarantee will create an obligation only if there is a default. Derivatives are a form of off-balance sheet transaction.

Operational risk: its largest definition says it includes all the risks not included in market risks and credit risks. This includes losses arising from fraud, failure in computer systems and data entry errors.

Option: a contract that gives the holder the right to buy or sell a specific number of commodities or securities at a stated price and date in the future.

Over-the-counter: refers to a trade between two financial institutions.

P/E ratio: this ratio is defined as the current price per share divided by the earnings per share.

Plain vanilla: refers to the simplest version of a financial product, such as options.

Position: refers to the type of risks taken on a specific market. For instance, as concerns interest rate risk, do you benefit when the interest rate goes up or when the interest rate goes down?

Profit centre: part of a bank for which both revenue and cost are allocated so that a profit can be calculated. A profit centre could be a product, a department such as a branch, or a client relationship.

Provisions for credit risk: represent the reduction in value of a loan due to the likelihood of delinquency. Provisions are an expense in the P&L at the time it is created. Accumulated provisions on loans appear as a reduction in the gross value of loans in the balance sheet. Specific provisions refer to likely losses identified on a specific transaction. General provisions are not linked to any specific transactions but are created by the accountant as a general reserve.

Put option: the right to sell an asset at a specific date in the future at a predetermined price (the exercise price).

RAROC: risk-adjusted return on capital. It is defined as the profit allocated to a profit centre divided by the equity allocated to that profit centre. It can be interpreted as the return on equity (ROE) of a profit centre.

Rating: refers to the credit quality of a counterparty. External ratings are given by rating agencies (ranging from AAA very safe asset to C). Internal ratings are granted by the bank itself.

Recourse: with reference to asset sales with recourse. In the context of a sale of a loan by a bank to investors, these have the right to call the guarantee from the bank should the borrower be unable to meet their obligations.

Recovery rate: the proportion of the promised payment that is recovered when a borrower defaults. It could come from the residual value of a borrower's assets from a guarantee.

Reinsurance: company that specializes in insuring the risks of other insurance companies.

Replacement risk: the risk that a counterparty defaults in a derivative contract, and that you need to buy or sell the asset at an unfavourable price prevailing on the market at that time.

Repricing gap: the difference between short-term assets that are repriced over a certain interval and the deposits that are repriced over the same time period. A positive gap indicates an excess of assets, while a negative gap indicates an excess of deposits.

Return on equity = earnings after tax divided by equity. This ratio is one of the most important drivers of the value of shares.

ROE: *see* return on equity.

Run: *see* bank run.

RWA: risk-weighted asset defined as the book value of assets multiplied by a weight to reflect the riskiness of the asset.

Securitization: the process of transformation of a bank loan into tradable securities. It often involves the creation of a separate corporate entity, the special purpose vehicle (SPV), which buys the loans, financing itself with securities that are sold to investors.

Settlement risk: between two counterparties, the risk that a counterparty to whom a firm has made a delivery of assets or money defaults before the amount due or assets have been received.

Simulation model: a computer-based tool that generates potential income statements and balance sheets for different sets of assumptions, such as the interest rate curve, volume of business or sensitivity of rates.

Special purpose vehicle: a legal corporate entity created to buy loans from banks. It finances itself with securities issued to investors.

SPV: *see* special purpose vehicle.

Standard deviation: a statistical measure of the average degree of variation of a random variable from its average value.

Supplementary capital: *see* Tier 2.

Swaps: an agreement between two parties to exchange interest payments (for instance, fixed versus floating) over a certain period of time. The interest is calculated on the notional principle.

Synthetic instrument: a combination of two or several financial instruments that replicate the cash flows of another instrument.

Systemic risk: the risk that a failure causes widespread difficulties in the financial system as a whole.

Tier 1: the capital recognized for the Cooke BIS ratio is composed of two parts: tier 1 and tier 2. Tier 1 (also called core capital) essentially incorporates the shareholders' equity reported in the book plus general provisions.

Tier 2: incorporates various items such as the re-evaluation of real estates, part of excessive specific provisions, unrealized gains on securities (weighted at 45%) and subordinated debt (limited to 50% of tier 1). Also called supplementary capital.

Trading book: bank activities are classified into two groups: banking book and trading book. The trading book includes derivative trades such as options, futures, treasury bonds. Its key characteristic is that the value of the book is calculated every day. This is referred to as marked-to-market.

Trading portfolio: refers to the part of the bond portfolio that a bank intends to trade in the short term. In most countries, it must be marked-to-market.

Transaction costs: the costs incurred in trading.

Value centre: *see* profit centre.

Value creation: the difference between the value of an investment and the amount of money invested by shareholders.

Value-at-risk: refers to the potential adverse change in the value of an asset or of a portfolio of assets.

VAR: *see* value-at-risk.

Volatility: refers to the potential magnitude of a change in interest rates, currency or prices. It is often measured with the statistical 'standard deviation'.

Writer: refers to the seller or issuer of an option.

Yield curve: set of interest rates with different maturities at a specific point in time.

Zero coupon bond: a bond that pays one single payment at the maturity of the bond.

Zero coupon spot rate: interest rate observed today on a zero coupon bond.

Appendix

REFERENCES

Jean Dermine's publications on ALM-related topics include the following.

Pricing Policies of Financial Intermediaries, Springer Verlag (Studies in Contemporary Economics n° 5), Berlin. Laureate of the 1984 BACOB Prize for Economic and Financial Research, 1984.

'Taxes, inflation and banks' market values', *Journal of Business, Finance and Accounting*, 12 (1), 1985.

'The measurement of interest rate risk by financial intermediaries', *Journal of Bank Research*, Summer, 1985.

'Accounting framework for banks, a market value approach', *SUERF Series*, 50 A, 1985.

'Deposit rates, credit rates and bank capital, the Klein-Monti model revisited', *Journal of Banking and Finance*, 10, 1986.

'Measuring the market value of a bank, a primer', *Finance* 8, 1987.

'Duration and taxes, an application of Paul Samuelson's tax rate invariance theorem', mimeo, INSEAD, 1991.

'Floating rate securities and duration, a note', mimeo, INSEAD, 1991.

'The BIS proposal for the measurement of interest rate risk, some pitfalls', *Journal of International Securities Markets*, 1991.

'Deposit rate ceilings and the market value of banks, the case of France 1971–1981', *Journal of Money, Credit and Banking* (with P. Hillion), 1992.

'The international regulation of interest rate risk, some pitfalls', in *Risk-Based Capital Regulations, Asset Management and Funding Strategies*, Stone Ed., Business One Irwin, 1993.

'The evaluation of interest rate risk, some warnings about the Basle proposal', *Finanzmarkt und Portfolio Management*, 7, 1993.

'Loan arbitrage-free pricing', *The Financier*, 2(2), 1995.

'Loan valuation, a modern finance perspective', mimeo, INSEAD, 1996.

'Pitfalls in the application of RAROC, with reference to loan management', *The Arbitrageur–The Financier*, 1(1), 1998.

'Unexpected inflation and bank stock returns, the case of France 1977–1991', *Journal of Banking and Finance*, 23 (6) (with F. Lajéri), 1999.

'DCF vs real options how best to value online: financial companies? (with an application to Egg)', INSEAD case series (with K. Wildberger and H. Georgeson), 2001.

'Credit risk and the deposit insurance premium, a note', *Journal of Economics and Business* (with F. Lajéri), 2001.

'ALM for banks' in *Handbook of Asset and Liability Modeling*, eds S. Zenios and W. Ziemba, North Holland, forthcoming.

Additional publications by Jean Dermine can be found on his personal page at *www.INSEAD.edu*.

Useful references can be found on the Bank for International Settlements' website: *www.bis.org*.

INDEX

accounting rules 71–2
accrual (banking) book 71–2, 136
American options 136
ask rate 2, 29–32
asset and liability committee (ALCO) 4, 136
asset and liability management (ALM) 4, 107–11, 136
Asset Liability Management Association (ALMA) 136
assets 2–3
  weighing rules 38
Association Française de Gestion Actif Passif (AFGAP) 136
average return 6–7

balance sheet 2–3, 12, 26–7
Bank for International Settlements (BIS) 36, 136
bank runs 99, 136
banking book 71–2, 136
banks
  assets 2–3
  flows of funds 2–4
  ROE breakdown 11–17
  services 1–4
  solvency 92
  sources of funds 2–3
  value creation 5–10, 66, 108–9
basis point 136
basis risk 79, 136
Basle Committee on Banking Supervision 36, 37, 49, 136
Basle II 49, 137
bid rate 2, 29–32
BIS ratio 36–8, 46, 137
book value of equity 92, 137
break-even loan pricing 44–6, 67

break-even loan rate 44–5, 52–3
break-even margin 45–6

call options 103–4, 137
capital
  economic capital 46–8, 49, 139
  Tier 1 and Tier 2 37, 38, 144
capital adequacy regulation 35–41, 46
capital ratio 137
cash flow 137
  liquidity gap 98–9
certificates of deposit (CDs) 137
clearing house 137
collateral 137
commodities 39–40, 137
confidence level 74–5, 137
contingent claims 3–4, 137
  see also forwards; futures; options
convexity 137
Cooke capital ratio 36–8, 46, 137
core capital 37, 38, 144
correlation 138
cost of debt (COD) 13–14, 137
cost of equity (COE) 6–7, 21, 137
  value creation 7–9, 108–9
cost-income ratio 13, 138
corporate tax rate 13–14
counterparty 138
counterparty risk 85, 86, 138
credit conversion factor 39
credit equivalent risk 39–40, 138
credit risk 38, 138
  diversification 61
  loan pricing 51–8, 109
credit risk provisions 53–5, 67, 142
cumulative gap 73
current exposure method 40

defeasance period 74, 138
delivery date 84, 85, 86, 138
deposits 3
    interest margin 30
    profitability of 26–9
derivatives 39, 138
    see also forwards; futures; options
discount rate 7–9, 138
discounting 93, 138
diversification
    credit risk 61
    funding sources 99
duration 92–4, 138

earnings-at-risk (EAR) 73–4, 138
    in 'normal' times 74–5
    under 'stress' scenarios 75
earnings-on-assets (EOA) 13–14, 139
economic capital 46–8, 49, 139
    allocation 47–8
economic profit (EP) see economic
        value added
economic value added (EVA) 21–2, 66,
        109, 139
economic value of equity 139
efficiency ratio (cost-income ratio) 13, 138
equity 2–3, 139
    allocation 20–2, 46, 47–8, 67
    investment 7–9, 66, 108
'equity' spread 43–50, 61
European options 139
exchange 139
exercise date 139
exercise price 103, 104, 139
expected return on a bank share 6–7
expiration date 139

fair value 54, 71, 139
financial futures 85–7, 102, 103, 140
flows of funds 2–4
forward rate 140
forwards 84–5, 102, 140

future exchange 85–6
futures 85–7, 102, 103, 140

gaps see liquidity gap; repricing gaps
general provisions 37, 142
gross revenue 140
guarantees 39, 140

haircut 140
hedging 87
holding period 74, 140

institutional investors 60, 140
International Monetary Fund (IMF) 37
income statement 12
interbank rate 2, 140
    transfer pricing 28–32
interest margin 30, 140
interest rate risk 69–81, 110, 140
    measuring 70–2
    reporting 74–5
    repricing gap 72–4
    simulation model 77–81
    two measures of 94–5
    value of equity at risk 91–6
inverted yield curve 140
investment portfolio 71, 140

leverage (gearing) 14, 141
liabilities 2–3
LIBID 140
LIBOR 140
liquidity 61, 86
liquidity gap 98–9, 141
liquidity ratio 99
liquidity risk 86, 97–100, 110, 141
loan pricing 67, 109
    credit risk and credit provisions 51–8
    'equity' spread 43–50, 61
loans
    interest margin 30
    profitability of 26–9
    securitization 46, 59–63, 67, 110, 143

long position 86
loss given default (LGD) 141

margin 86, 141
margin calls 86, 141
market-to-book value ratio 141
market risks 71
market value of shares 7–9, 66, 108, 141
marking-to-market 71, 86, 141
matched maturity marginal value of
    fund (matched maturity interbank
    rate) (MMMVF) 29, 30–1
matching maturity rule 28–9
maturity 28–9, 93, 141
Monte Carlo simulation 79, 141

net interest margin (NIM) 30, 71, 95, 141
net loan value 54, 57–8
netting 141
note issuance facilities (NIFs) 39, 142
notional 142
novation 85, 142

off balance sheet 3–4, 142
    weighting system 39–40
    see also forwards; futures; options
operating expenses (OE) ratio 13–14
operational risk 142
options 101–6, 142
over-the-counter 142

P/E ratio 142
plain vanilla 142
position 86, 142
profit
    allocation 20–2, 25–33
    economic see economic value added
    on a loan 54, 58
profit centres 19–23, 66–7, 109, 142
profitability
    deposits and loans 26-9
    interest rate fluctuations and 70

provisions for credit risk 53–5, 67, 142
put options 104, 142

RAROC (risk-adjusted return on
    capital) 20–1, 143
rating 60, 143
rating agencies 60, 61
recourse 39, 143
recovery rate 143
regulatory capital ratio 36–8, 46, 137
re-insurance companies 60, 143
replacement risk 85, 143
repricing gaps (bucket) 72–4, 143
    hedging with futures 87
    limits to use of 78–9
reserve requirement 2, 3, 29–32
return on equity (ROE) 7–9, 108–9, 143
    breakdown 11–17
risk
    basis risk 79, 136
    credit risk see credit risk
    interest rate risk see interest rate risk
    liquidity risk 86, 97–100, 110, 141
    market risks 71
    operational risk 142
    option risk 104–5
    replacement risk 85, 143
    settlement risk 143
    systemic risk 144
risk-based capital (economic capital) 46–8,
    49, 139
risk premium 6–7
risk-weighted assets (RWA) 38, 143

securitization 46, 59–63, 67, 110, 143
settlement risk 143
short position 86
simulation model 77–81, 143
software 113–15
special purpose vehicle (SPV) 60, 61, 144
standard deviation 144
standardized contracts 86
'stress' scenarios 75, 99

supplementary capital 37, 38, 144
swaps 144
synthetic instrument 144
systemic risk 144

tax rate 13–14
Tier One capital 37, 38, 144
Tier Two capital 37, 38, 144
trading book 71–2, 144
trading portfolio (treasury portfolio) 71, 144
transaction costs 144
transfer price 25–33, 67, 109
treasury portfolio (trading portfolio) 71, 144

value-at-risk (VAR) 92–4, 144
value-based management 9
value centres *see* profit centres
value creation 65–7, 108–10, 144
   banks 5–10, 66, 108–9

loan management 67
   profit centres 20–2, 66–7
   zero 45
value of equity at risk 91–6
volatility 144
   interest rate 74–5, 110
   options and 104–5

weighting
   rules for assets 38
   system for off-balance sheet items 39–40
World Bank 37
writer (options) 103, 104, 145

yield curve 76, 145

zero coupon bond 145
zero coupon spot rate 145

LICENSING AGREEMENT

This book comes with a CD Rom software package. By opening this package you are agreeing to be bound by the following:

CD-ROM Copyright notice

Disclaimer

IMPORTANT – READ CAREFULLY

b) The Licensee may not assign or sub-licence any of its rights or obligations under this Agreement without the prior written consent of the Publishers.

c) This Agreement is governed by the law of England and the parties accept the exclusive jurisdiction of the English courts.

2. GRANT OF LICENCE

Single Computer Use. This Agreement permits the Licensee to use one copy of the Product on a single computer for search and retrieval purposes only. Once the Licensee has run that portion of the Product which set-up or installs the Product on the Licensee's computer, the Licensee may only use the Product on a different computer if the files installed by the set-up or installation program from the first computer (if any) are first deleted. The Licensee may not copy the contents or any part of the Product from the Product to a computer hard disk or any other permanent electronic storage device (except as occurs when the Licensee runs the set-up/install program or uses other features of the Product on a single computer).

For the avoidance of doubt, the Product shall remain the exclusive property of the Publishers at all times.

3. PROPRIETARY RIGHTS IN THE PRODUCT

Copyright and all intellectual property rights in the Product including in any images, photographs, animation, videos, audio, music, software and text incorporated in the Product is owned by the Publishers or their suppliers and is protected by United Kingdom copyright laws and international treaty provisions and the Licensee acknowledges that it has no rights therein except as set out in this Agreement.

4. OTHER RESTRICTIONS

The Licensee may not:

I) pass free of charge, or sell, name and address information from the Product to any third party;

II) duplicate, transfer, sell, rent, lease or commercially exploit the Product or information contained therein.

III) alter, merge, or adapt the Product or any part thereof in any way including dissembling or decompiling except as permitted by law.

5. WARRANTY

The Publishers warrant that the Product will substantially conform to the applicable user documentation accompanying the Product and also that the CD-ROM media on which the Product is distributed is free from defects in materials and workmanship. The Publishers will replace defective media at no charge, provided that the Licensee returns the Product with dated proof of payment to the Publishers at 128 Long Acre, London WC2E 9AN within 30 days of receipt. These are the Licensee's sole remedies for any breach of these warranties.

Although the information contained in the Product has been prepared with reasonable care the Publishers do not warrant the accuracy or completeness of the Product or the results to be obtained therefrom. The Publishers do not warrant that the Licensee's use of the product will be uninterrupted or error free. Any implied warranties on the Product are limited to 30 days from the date of receipt.

While the Publishers have used all reasonable endeavours to ensure that the software they have written is Year 2000 compliant it is not possible to ensure that software and systems supplied by third parties are Year 2000 compliant and accordingly no guarantees are given in that respect and all warranties, whether express or implied (whether arising statutorily or otherwise), are hereby excluded to the maximum extent permitted by law.

EXCEPT AS EXPRESSLY PROVIDED IN THIS AGREEMENT the Publishers disclaim all other warranties either express or implied including but not limited to implied warranties of satisfactory quality or fitness for a particular purpose with respect to the Product, accompanying materials and any accompanying literature to the maximum extent permitted by law.

6. LIMITATION OF LIABILITY

To the maximum extent permitted by law, in no event shall the Publishers or its suppliers be liable for any damages whatsoever including without limitation special, indirect or consequential loss, damages for loss of business, lost profits, business interruption or other pecuniary loss arising from the use or inability to use the Product, even if advised of the possibility of such damages. In no case shall the Publishers' liability exceed the fee paid by the Licensee save that nothing in clauses 5 or 6 of this Agreement affects any rights the Licensee may have against the Publishers for death or personal injury caused by the Publishers' negligence.

7. TERMINATION

This Agreement may be terminated by either party if the other is in material breach of this Agreement and has failed to rectify such breach within 30 days of receipt notice of the same.

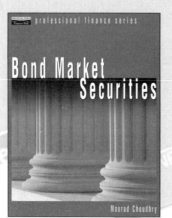
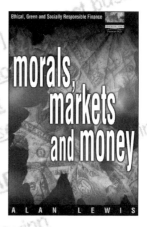
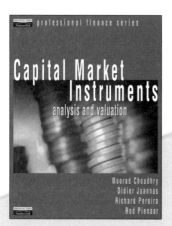